ANNE WILLAN'S
LOOK&COOK

Meat Classics

ANNE WILLAN'S
LOOK & COOK

Meat Classics

DORLING KINDERSLEY
LONDON • NEW YORK • STUTTGART

A DORLING KINDERSLEY BOOK

Created and Produced by
CARROLL & BROWN LIMITED
5 Lonsdale Road
London NW6 6RA

Editorial Director Jeni Wright
Editors Jennifer Feller
Norma MacMillan
Sally Poole
Stella Vayne

Art Editor Vicky Zentner
Designers Lucy De Rosa
Lyndel Donaldson
Wendy Rogers
Mary Staples
Lisa Webb

First published in Great Britain in 1992
by Dorling Kindersley Limited
9 Henrietta Street, London WC2E 8PS

A CIP catalogue record for this book is available
from the British Library
ISBN 0-86318-989-X

Reproduced by Colourscan, Singapore
Printed and bound in Italy by A. Mondadori, Verona

CONTENTS

MEAT

THE LOOK & COOK APPROACH

Welcome to **Meat Classics,** and the *Look & Cook* series. These volumes are designed to be the simplest, most informative cookbooks you'll ever own. They are the closest I can come to sharing my techniques for cooking my own favourite recipes without actually being with you in the kitchen looking over your shoulder.

Equipment and ingredients often determine whether or not you can cook a particular dish, so *Look & Cook* illustrates everything you need at the beginning of each recipe. You'll see at a glance how long a recipe takes to cook, how many servings it makes, what the finished dish looks like, and how much preparation can be done ahead. When you start to cook, you'll find the preparation and cooking are organized into easy-to-follow steps. Each stage is colour-coded and everything is shown in photographs with brief text to go with each step. You will never be in doubt about what it is you are doing, why you are doing it, or how it should look.

EQUIPMENT

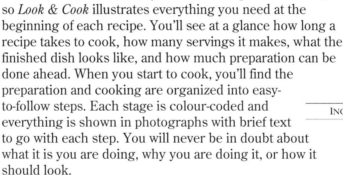

INGREDIENTS

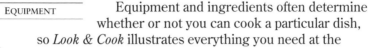

🍽 SERVES 4   🥣 WORK TIME 15-20 MINUTES   ♨ COOKING TIME 20-25 MINUTES

I've also included helpful hints and ideas under "Anne Says". These may list an alternative ingredient or piece of equipment, or sometimes the reason for using a certain method is explained, or there is some advice on mastering a particular technique. Similarly, if there is a crucial stage in a recipe when things can go wrong, I've included some warnings called "Take Care".

Many of the photographs are annotated to pinpoint why certain pieces of equipment work best, or how the food should look at that stage of cooking. Because presentation is so important, a picture of the finished dish and serving suggestions are at the end of each recipe.

Thanks to all this information, you can't go wrong. I'll be with you every step of the way. So please, come with me into the kitchen to look, cook, and create some delicious **Meat Classics.**

Anne Willan

WHY MEAT?

Nutritious and full of flavour, meat has long been a centrepiece for festive and family menus. Meat adapts to many different styles of cooking which are found worldwide, though individual cuts may vary from country to country and even region to region. The great variety of beef, veal, lamb, and pork offers a choice to please every taste.

RECIPE CHOICE

The different cuts and types of meat available offer an almost limitless number of dishes. You'll find here an international assortment, from Mexican Barbecued Pork with Salsa, and Turkish Minced Lamb Kebabs, to Japanese Pork and Ginger Sukiyaki, with an array of traditional and contemporary techniques and ingredients to match. I've divided the book into two sections, for quick and slow cooking. Quickly cooked meat dishes require less than an hour, so they are perfect for busy evenings. For example, Russian Beef Sauté can be ready in about 35 minutes. More slowly cooked meat dishes include stews that simmer gently in the oven, such as Provençal Beef Stew, and roasts such as Roast Leg of Lamb with Haricot Beans.

QUICK COOKING

Turkish Minced Lamb Kebabs: lamb and herb mixture is shaped into cylinders and cooked on skewers to serve with a cool cucumber and yogurt sauce. *Indian Minced Lamb Kebabs:* spicy kebabs are served with cucumber salad. *Mexican Barbecued Pork with Salsa:* loin of pork, marinated in pungent barbecue sauce, is grilled to serve with crisp tortilla strips and salsa. *Barbecued Steak:* steak, basted with barbecue sauce while grilling, has an accompaniment of salsa. *Russian Beef Sauté:* tender strips of beef and mushrooms are complemented by a tangy soured cream and mustard sauce. *Beef Sauté with Paprika:* strips of red pepper and paprika add colour to the beef. *Veal Escalopes with Sage and Parma Ham:* veal escalopes, topped with Parma ham and fresh sage leaves, are sautéed in butter. *Veal Piccate with Mushrooms and Marsala:* small escalopes are served in a rich sauce. *Pork and Ginger Sukiyaki:* slices of pork are perfumed with ginger, then cooked sukiyaki-style with mushrooms and spring onions in soy sauce and sake wine. *Beef, Ginger, and Sesame Sukiyaki:* sesame oil and a sprinkling of sesame seeds add a nutty flavour and fragrance to traditional beef sukiyaki. *Rack of Lamb with Sautéed Cucumbers and Mint:* sautéed cucumbers are an unusual addition to the traditional combination of roast lamb with mint. *Rack of Lamb Coated with Parsley and Breadcrumbs:* a crispy coating of parsley and buttered breadcrumbs covers succulent rack of lamb. *Minute Steak Marchand de Vin:* delicate steaks cut from the fillet are fried in a heavy-based pan and served with a simple sauce of red wine and shallots. *Minute Steak Dijonnaise:* tangy Dijon mustard and cream flavour the golden sauce for minute steaks. *Butterflied Leg of Lamb:* boned leg of lamb is laid flat and marinated in garlic and herbs, then grilled. *Butterflied Loin of Pork:* garlic, herbs, and mustard infuse boneless loin of pork, opened flat for grilling. *Lamb Chops in Paper Cases with Fennel:* browned loin chops on a bed of fennel and tomatoes bake gently in a paper case. *Lamb Chops in Paper Cases with Leeks:* sautéed leeks, tomatoes, and herbs complement lamb chops baked in paper.

SLOW COOKING

Fillet of Beef Stuffed with Mushrooms: for a grand occasion, a whole fillet is stuffed with a "duxelles" mixture of chopped mushrooms, parsley, garlic, and bacon, and served with a Madeira sauce. *Tournedos of Beef with Mushrooms:* thick fillet steaks, spread with mushroom "duxelles", are served on rounds of turnip and topped with Madeira sauce. *Roast Leg of Lamb with Haricot Beans:* garlic-studded leg of lamb is served Brittany-style with haricot beans and baked tomatoes. *Lemon Roast Leg of Lamb with Courgette Gratins:* slivers of lemon zest and garlic spike the lamb, which is served with baked courgette and Gruyère gratins. *Italian Braised Veal:* the classic Milanese "osso buco" is topped with a zesty "gremolata" of parsley, lemon zest, and garlic. *French Braised Lamb:* tomato, garlic, and fresh rosemary top knuckles of lamb braised in a red wine sauce. *Aunt Sally's Meat Loaf:* here an all-round favourite is made with minced beef and veal, bacon, spinach, and fresh herbs, spiced with Worcestershire sauce. *Pork Loaf with Apricots:* in this sweet and savoury variation a layer of dried apricots is added to a pork-based meat loaf.

Roast Leg of Pork with Orange: leg of pork is cooked slowly, basted with fresh orange juice, then glazed and topped with slices of orange and cloves, and served with a spiced Grand Marnier sauce. *Roast Leg of Pork with Apples:* the pork is basted with apple juice and served with baked apples stuffed with brown sugar and sultanas. *Indian Braised Lamb:* cubes of lamb are gently cooked in spiced yogurt and cream in this fragrant dish. *Moroccan Spiced Lamb:* a change of spice and a toasted almond topping give the lamb a Moroccan flavour. *Roast Rib of Beef Pebronata:* juicy beef rib roast is served with a brilliant red pepper and tomato sauce from Corsica. *Roast Rib of Beef with Yorkshire Pudding:* traditional Sunday lunch of tender beef and golden Yorkshire puddings is served with a rich gravy. *Roast Rib of Beef with Glazed Onions, Turnips, and Carrots:* vegetables glazed with butter and sugar make a winter garnish for rib of beef. *Provençal Beef Stew:* in this country "daube", beef is simmered in red wine with bacon, salt pork, herbs, garlic, black olives, and zest of orange.

Provençal Lamb Stew with Green Olives: in this variation cubes of lamb replace beef, with green olives instead of black. *Chilli con Carne:* Texas-style chilli is made with tender beef, tomatoes, and lots of spice. *Mexican Chilli con Carne:* Chilli goes "south of the border", with the addition of chocolate, plus cinnamon and cloves. *Burgundy Pot Roast:* classic Burgundian garnish of bacon, small onions, and mushrooms is perfect with beef pot-roasted in red wine. *Flemish Pot Roast with Beer:* beer, carrots, and lots of onions give a good flavour to beef pot roast. *French Hot Pot (Pot-au-Feu):* a French country favourite of beef simmered with aromatic vegetables to spoon-cutting tenderness, and a separate course of rich broth. *Potée:* this pork hot pot is cooked with smoked bacon and cabbage wedges. *Pork Noisettes with Cornbread and Cranberries:* thick pork noisettes with a cornbread, pecan, and celery stuffing are accompanied by a tart cranberry and wine sauce. *Pork Noisettes with Cornbread and Apple Rings:* stuffed noisettes are served with a creamy sauce and caramelized apple rings. *Steak and Wild Mushroom Pie:* cubes of steak cooked with meaty wild mushrooms are topped with a quick puff pastry crust. *Individual Victorian Steak and Kidney Pies:* kidneys and oysters are added to the steak filling in these individual pies. *Hungarian Beef Goulash:* a hearty beef and pepper stew, highly flavoured with paprika and caraway seeds, with tiny dumplings. *Hungarian Veal Goulash:* chunks of veal, potatoes, and green peppers are cooked in a pungent paprika, garlic, and tomato sauce.

EQUIPMENT

Meat cuts and techniques vary widely, but the list of specialized equipment needed to execute them is short. You'll need a chef's knife for trimming and cutting meat into pieces, whether cubes or slices. For boning, use a boning knife; the sharp tip of the blade allows you to manoeuvre around the bone without losing too much flesh, and the handle is shaped for a firm grip. All knives should be sharpened on a steel each time you use them. For carving, a knife with a flexible blade is helpful, long or short depending on the cut.

Stews and slow-cooked meat dishes demand an assortment of casseroles and saucepans with lids. Roasting tins in medium and large sizes are required for browning and roasting, and a sauté pan or large frying pan is needed for sautés. An oval pie dish is classic for the steak pie, and you'll need parchment paper for lamb chops in paper cases and metal skewers for lamb kebabs. A meat thermometer comes in handy for testing the temperature of cooked meat, but a metal skewer also works well. Use an electric or hand mincer for mincing beef, lamb, or pork, with a food processor as an alternative; or save time and ask your butcher to prepare the meat for you. Cooking meat on a barbecue adds a smoky flavour, but your grill is quite acceptable as a substitute.

INGREDIENTS

Meat often stands alone as a roast, or grilled chop or steak. The many ingredients which act as partners tend to be a foil for the full flavour of the meat itself.

Fresh herbs such as parsley, thyme, coriander, oregano, sage, and the classic partners for lamb, rosemary and mint, nicely complement meat, whether in stews or roasted. A wide variety of spices, such as cayenne, cinnamon, coriander seeds, cloves, caraway seeds, chilli powder, ginger, mace, nutmeg, cumin, paprika, cardamom, and turmeric add depth and often international flavour. The allium family – onion, garlic, and shallot – is essential to many dishes, while olives and piquant aromatics, such as chillies and fresh root ginger, add distinctive taste to others. Mustard provides good balance in various sauces as well as being an excellent coating for pork.

"Meat and vegetables" has become a catchphrase, whether you think of carrots, celery, leeks, or tomatoes to flavour a sauce, or mushrooms, fennel, peppers, or cucumbers as the finishing touch. Fruit, from apples and oranges to apricots and cranberries, is a tasty, juicy addition to meat dishes, particularly succulent pork. Even chocolate appears in a sauce for beef, while black treacle adds sweetness to barbecued

pork and brown sugar coats roast leg of pork. Crumbly cornbread does double duty as a stuffing for pork noisettes and the accompaniment to chilli.

The flavour of meat is often intensified by the addition of beef or veal stock. As for alcohol, wine, whether red or white, is a natural partner for meat, and Madeira, pastis, sake, mirin, and even Grand Marnier, blend well in savoury sauces and glazes. Beer and fruit juices appear in many regional meat dishes. Milk products, such as soured cream and double cream, add richness and smooth taste to sauces for meats; yogurt acts as the cooking liquid and tenderizer in Indian braised lamb.

TECHNIQUES

The different meats in these recipes call for an assortment of useful techniques. You will learn how to trim large cuts of excess fat and sinew before cooking, and how to cut meat into large cubes for stew or smaller pieces for chilli – the size must be uniform to ensure even cooking. You will see how to carve neat minute steaks and the thin slices needed for pork sukiyaki, how to mince meat, and how to pound escalopes or medallions to very thin slices for quicker cooking. A few more advanced methods of preparing meat include preparing rack of lamb, and butterflying a leg of lamb by removing the bones and cutting the meat so it will lie flat.

Cooking methods for meat are diverse: even the style for a simple stew can differ. For some, cubes of meat are first browned to lock in juices before simmering in flavoured liquid; in others, the meat pieces are added raw and cooked long and gently to tenderize them and produce a rich sauce. Large pieces of meat may be simmered whole in plenty of liquid or they may be pot-roasted by cooking them in their own juices with a small amount of stock until very tender. Tender cuts are usually roasted; you will learn the method of searing them in a very hot oven to form a browned crust, then reducing the temperature to cook the meat thoroughly; you will also learn to check whether the meat is done using a skewer or a meat thermometer.

For quickly cooked meats the popular methods of pan-frying and grilling are explained. From small strips of beef to veal escalopes and beef steaks, pan-frying is simple and fast, preserving flavour and tenderness. Grilling quickly cooks a variety of meats from steaks to butterflied leg of lamb, first marinated to ensure juiciness. A more unusual technique is used for lamb chops in paper cases. Here the cooking must be carefully timed so the lamb is perfectly done in its container of parchment paper.

TURKISH MINCED LAMB KEBABS

Sis Köfte

 SERVES 6   WORK TIME 30-35 MINUTES   COOKING TIME 10-15 MINUTES

EQUIPMENT

chef's knife

small knife   pastry brush

wooden spoon

large metal spoon

palette knife

6 metal skewers

colander   food processor*

bowls

small frying pan

grater

chopping board

*mincer can also be used

Lamb is the traditional Mediterranean meat, and each country from Morocco to Greece has its own specialities. In Turkey, minced lamb is mixed with onion, garlic, and cumin, formed into cylinders around skewers as kebabs, and grilled.

GETTING AHEAD

The minced meat mixture and yogurt sauce can be made up to 8 hours ahead and kept covered in the refrigerator; the flavours will mellow. The kebabs are best cooked just before serving.

metric	SHOPPING LIST	imperial
1 kg	boned lamb shoulder	2 lb
1	large onion	1
3	garlic cloves	3
3-5	sprigs of fresh mint	3-5
3-5	sprigs of parsley	3-5
10 ml	ground cumin	2 tsp
	salt and pepper	
	olive oil, for brushing	
	For the yogurt sauce	
1	large cucumber	1
5 ml	salt	1 tsp
1	garlic clove	1
500 ml	plain yogurt	16 fl oz

INGREDIENTS

boned lamb shoulder

cucumber

plain yogurt   onion

parsley   olive oil

ground cumin   garlic cloves

fresh mint

ORDER OF WORK

1 MAKE THE YOGURT SAUCE

2 PREPARE THE MINCED MEAT MIXTURE

3 PREPARE AND COOK THE KEBABS

1 MAKE THE YOGURT SAUCE

1 Wipe and trim the cucumber. Grate the cucumber, with the skin, into a large bowl. Stir in the salt well, so that it is evenly distributed.

Press cucumber firmly against large holes as you grate into big bowl

Green skin adds colour to grated cucumber

2 Set the colander over a bowl. Transfer the grated cucumber to the colander and let drain 10 minutes to draw out excess moisture.

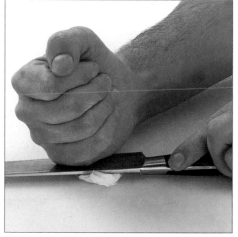

3 Set the flat side of the chef's knife on top of the garlic clove and strike it with your fist. Discard the skin and finely chop the garlic.

4 Put the yogurt in a large bowl. Remove more water from the cucumber by squeezing it in your hand. Add the cucumber to the yogurt. Stir in the garlic with salt to taste. Cover and chill.

2 PREPARE THE MINCED MEAT MIXTURE

1 Trim any fat and sinew from the lamb. Cut the meat into small chunks. Peel and trim the onion and cut it into chunks.

2 Work the chunks of lamb and onion in the food processor, in batches if necessary, until smooth, 1-2 minutes. Put the lamb and onion into a large bowl.

ANNE SAYS
"Do not overwork the lamb in the processor, or the kebabs will be tough."

3 Set the flat side of the chef's knife on top of each garlic clove and strike it with your fist. Discard the skin and finely chop the garlic. Strip the mint and parsley leaves from the stalks, reserving 6 mint leaves for garnish, and pile them on the chopping board. Finely chop the leaves.

4 Add the cumin, salt and pepper, garlic, and herbs to the meat. Beat with the wooden spoon until all the ingredients are thoroughly combined, 1-2 minutes.

5 To test the mixture for seasoning, fry a spoonful of the meat mixture in the small frying pan until browned on both sides. Taste, and add more salt and pepper to the uncooked mixture if necessary.

To adjust seasoning, fry small piece of mixture and taste

3 PREPARE AND COOK THE KEBABS

1 Heat the grill and set the rack 5 cm (2 inches) from the heat. Wet your hands and roll one-third of the mixture into a cylinder 2.5 cm (1 inch) in diameter. Repeat to make 2 more. Cut each cylinder into 6 equal lengths.

Meat is easy to shape and will not stick to your hands if they are damp

2 Brush the skewers and grill rack with olive oil. Thread the meat onto the skewers, pressing the cylinders well into shape; put the kebabs on the grill rack.

3 With the pastry brush, brush the kebabs with olive oil, and grill them until they are brown on top and sputtering, 5-7 minutes.

Be sure to brown meat on all sides

4 Turn the skewers and continue cooking until browned on the other side, 5-7 minutes longer. The meat should be well done but still juicy in the centre.

¶O¶   TO SERVE
Serve the kebabs on a bed of tabouleh salad, garnished with the reserved mint leaves, and decorated with tomatoes and black olives, if you like. Pass the yogurt sauce separately.

Kebabs are served sizzling on tabouleh salad

Cool yogurt sauce complements kebabs

VARIATION

INDIAN MINCED LAMB KEBABS

Additional spices and fresh coriander help transform these kebabs into an Indian feast.

1 In place of the yogurt sauce, make a cucumber and yogurt salad: peel and trim 2 large cucumbers, cut them in half, and scoop out the seeds with a teaspoon. Slice the cucumbers, omitting the salting and draining. Mix the cucumber with 250 ml (8 fl oz) plain yogurt, the finely chopped garlic, and salt to taste. Chill until serving.
2 Trim and mince the lamb and onion as directed in the main recipe. Finely chop the garlic. In place of the mint, chop the leaves from 3-5 sprigs of fresh coriander with the parsley.
3 Mix the minced meat and onion with the garlic, herbs, and cumin, adding 7.5 ml (1½ tsp) ground ginger, 10 ml (2 tsp) each ground turmeric and coriander, and 2.5 ml (½ tsp) ground cloves. Shape the mixture into 2.5 cm (1 inch) ovals, skewer, and cook as directed, 3-5 minutes per side.
4 Remove the kebabs from the skewers, if you like, and serve with the cucumber salad on a bed of saffron rice. Garnish with fresh coriander leaves.

MEXICAN BARBECUED PORK WITH SALSA

🍽 SERVES 6   🥣 WORK TIME 35-40 MINUTES*   ♨ COOKING TIME 40-50 MINUTES

EQUIPMENT

- rubber gloves
- greaseproof paper
- pastry brush
- paper towels
- chef's knife
- lemon squeezer
- bowls
- meat cleaver**
- small knife
- large metal spoon
- slotted spoon
- tongs
- sauté pan
- food processor***
- plate
- shallow dish
- frying pan
- rubber spatula

** heavy-based pan or rolling pin can also be used

*** blender can also be used

The barbecue sauce makes this pork taste as if cooked outdoors. Traditionally, fresh jalapeño peppers are used, but as their availability is limited, fresh green chillies make a good substitute.

*plus 2-8 hours marinating time

metric	SHOPPING LIST	imperial
1 kg	boned loin of pork	2 lb
3	ripe avocados	3
1	lemon	1
3	corn tortillas	3
75 ml	vegetable oil, more if needed	2½ fl oz
	For the salsa and barbecue sauce	
2	large onions	2
4	garlic cloves	4
3-4	sprigs of fresh coriander	3-4
2	fresh green chillies	2
1.15 kg	tomatoes	2½ lb
1	yellow or red pepper	1
1	lemon	1
	Tabasco sauce	
	salt	
45 ml	vegetable oil	3 tbsp
15 ml	coriander seeds	1 tbsp
4	limes	4
60 ml	red wine vinegar	4 tbsp
125 ml	black treacle	4 fl oz

INGREDIENTS

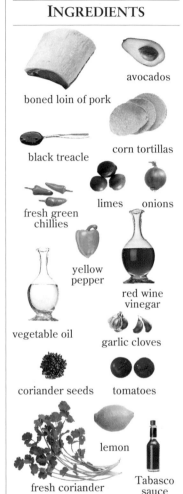

- boned loin of pork
- avocados
- black treacle
- corn tortillas
- fresh green chillies
- limes
- onions
- yellow pepper
- red wine vinegar
- vegetable oil
- garlic cloves
- coriander seeds
- tomatoes
- fresh coriander
- lemon
- Tabasco sauce

ORDER OF WORK

1. **MAKE THE SALSA AND BARBECUE SAUCE**

2. **PREPARE THE LOIN OF PORK**

3. **PREPARE THE GARNISH AND GRILL THE PORK**

1 MAKE THE SALSA AND BARBECUE SAUCE

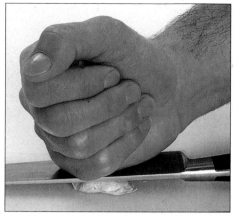

Coriander is delicate so chop coarsely to avoid bruising

1 Peel the onions, leaving a little of the root attached, and cut in half. Slice each half horizontally towards the root, leaving the slices attached at the root end, then slice vertically, again leaving the root end uncut. Cut across to make dice.

2 Set the flat side of the chef's knife on top of each garlic clove and strike it with your fist. Discard the skin and finely chop the garlic.

3 Strip the coriander leaves from the stalks, pile them on the chopping board, then finely chop the leaves. Core, deseed, and dice the chillies (see box, below).

HOW TO CORE, DESEED, AND DICE FRESH CHILLIES

Fresh chillies must be finely chopped so their heat spreads evenly through the dish. For a hotter flavour you can add the seeds, too. When handling chillies be sure to wear rubber gloves and to avoid contact with eyes, because the hot chillies can burn your hands and eyes.

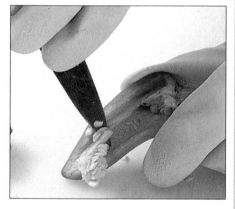

1 Cut the chillies lengthwise in half with a small knife.

2 Cut out the core and fleshy white "ribs" and scrape out the seeds.

3 Set each half cut-side up and slice it thinly lengthwise.

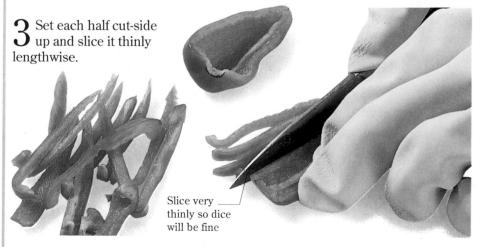

Slice very thinly so dice will be fine

4 Hold the strips together and cut across into very fine dice.

Contrasting textures are essence of salsa

Mingled cool and fiery flavours will stimulate tastebuds

4 Cut the cores from the tomatoes and score an "x" on the base of each with the tip of the small knife. Immerse in boiling water until the skin starts to split, 8-15 seconds. Transfer at once to a bowl of cold water. When cold, peel off the skin. Cut the tomatoes crosswise in half and squeeze out the seeds. Chop each half.

ANNE SAYS
"*A portion of these ingredients will be used for the salsa, the rest for the barbecue sauce.*"

5 To make the salsa, combine half of the onion, one-quarter of the garlic, the coriander, half of the chillies, and one-third of the tomatoes in a large bowl.

Yellow pepper adds crunchiness and texture to salsa

6 With a sharp movement, twist the core out of the pepper, then halve it, and scrape out the seeds. Cut away the white ribs on the inside. Set each half cut-side down on the work surface, flatten it with the heel of your hand, and slice lengthwise into strips. Gather the strips together in a pile and cut across into dice.

7 Add the diced pepper to the salsa ingredients. Squeeze the lemon and pour the juice into the salsa. Season to taste with Tabasco sauce and salt, then cover and refrigerate.

Freshly squeezed lime juice is delightfully aromatic

Coriander seeds introduce fragrant accent

8 To make the barbecue sauce, heat the oil in the sauté pan, add the remaining onion, garlic, and chillies, and sauté, stirring, until soft but not browned, 3-4 minutes. Add the coriander seeds and the remaining tomatoes. Squeeze the limes and pour the juice into the sauce.

9 Cook over medium heat, stirring occasionally, until reduced and thickened, about 15 minutes.

10 Add the red wine vinegar, bring to a boil, and reduce until thickened again, 8-10 minutes.

11 Stir in the black treacle and simmer the mixture 1-2 minutes longer. Season with salt.

12 Let the sauce cool slightly, then purée it in the food processor and let cool completely.

2 PREPARE THE LOIN OF PORK

1 Trim fat and any sinew from the pork and cut the meat across into 6 even slices. Put a slice between 2 sheets of greaseproof paper and flatten to a thickness of about 1 cm (½ inch) with the flat side of the meat cleaver. Put each remaining slice between greaseproof paper and flatten in the same way.

ANNE SAYS
"Flattening the meat ensures that it will cook quickly and evenly and not dry out."

Cut equal slices so pork cooks evenly

There is no need to trim off every thin sliver of fat

2 Put the pork slices into the shallow dish, cover with the cold barbecue sauce, and turn the meat so that it is thoroughly coated with the sauce. Cover the dish and then refrigerate at least 2 hours and up to 8 hours.

3 PREPARE THE GARNISH AND GRILL THE PORK

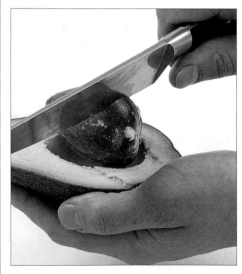

1 Heat the grill. Halve each avocado. With a chopping movement, imbed the blade of the chef's knife in each avocado stone and, twisting gently, lift it free. Or, scoop out the stones with a spoon.

2 Squeeze the lemon. With the small knife, peel the skin from each avocado half. Cut the halves crosswise into thin slices and lay them on the plate. Brush immediately with the lemon juice.

3 Stack the tortillas and cut them into 5 mm (¼ inch) strips. Heat the oil in the frying pan, add the tortilla strips, and fry over high heat, turning once, until crisp, 1-2 minutes. Keep warm on paper towels in a low oven.

4 Brush the grill rack with oil. Take each slice of pork from the barbecue sauce with the tongs, allowing excess sauce to drip off, and put on the grill rack. Cook about 5 cm (2 inches) from the heat until brown and slightly charred, 5-7 minutes.

Oiled rack keeps pork from sticking

5 Turn the meat slices over, brush each one with barbecue sauce, and cook until well browned and no longer pink inside, about 5-7 minutes.

ANNE SAYS
"The meat should feel firm when you press it with a finger."

¶©¶ TO SERVE
Transfer the grilled pork to warmed individual plates. Spoon some salsa onto a few salad leaves, if you like, and top with a herb sprig. Add the tortilla strips and avocado slices.

Avocado slices are cool contrast with spicy pork

VARIATION

BARBECUED STEAK
Here T-bone or sirloin steaks replace the pork for an equally delicious dish.

1 Prepare the salsa and barbecue sauce as directed.
2 Trim 6 T-bone or sirloin steaks of fat and any sinew; they should be about 2 cm (¾ inch) thick. Marinate the steaks in the barbecue sauce as directed. Omit the avocados and tortillas.
3 Heat the grill, and grill the steaks as directed, allowing 3-4 minutes for rare meat or 5-6 minutes for medium-done meat. Brush the tops of the steaks with more sauce as they cook. Turn the meat over, brush with more barbecue sauce, and cook 3-4 minutes for rare, 5-6 minutes for medium. When rare, the steak will feel spongy when pressed with a finger and medium meat will resist slightly when pressed.
4 Take the steaks from the heat and brush with a little more barbecue sauce. Serve with the salsa on a bed of fresh young spinach leaves with herb sprigs.

GETTING AHEAD
The salsa and barbecue sauce can be made 2-3 days in advance and kept, covered, in the refrigerator. The meat can be prepared and marinated up to 8 hours ahead, then grilled just before serving.

RUSSIAN BEEF SAUTE

EQUIPMENT

wooden spoon

slotted spoon

chef's knife

small knife

bowl

plate

sauté pan

paper towels

large plate

chopping board

This wonderfully quick main course is based on beef Stroganoff. The tang of soured cream and Dijon mustard complements the rich fillet of beef, and mushrooms are a welcome addition to the sauce, although not strictly authentic. Fresh noodles, tomato or plain, are a good accompaniment.

GETTING AHEAD
It is best not to prepare this dish in advance, because reheating may curdle the cream and overcook the beef.

INGREDIENTS

fillet of beef*

mushrooms   onions

fresh tarragon   soured cream

plain flour   butter

Dijon mustard

beef stock

vegetable oil

metric	SHOPPING LIST	imperial
750 g	fillet of beef	1½ lb
250 g	mushrooms	8 oz
2	medium onions	2
3-5	sprigs of fresh tarragon	3-5
30 g	butter, more if needed	1 oz
30 ml	vegetable oil	2 tbsp
	salt and pepper	
15 ml	plain flour	1 tbsp
125 ml	beef stock or water	4 fl oz
10-15 ml	Dijon mustard	2-3 tsp
125 ml	soured cream	4 fl oz

*top sirloin can be used

ORDER OF WORK

1 PREPARE THE BEEF AND SAUCE INGREDIENTS

2 COOK THE SAUTE

1 PREPARE THE BEEF AND SAUCE INGREDIENTS

1 Trim the beef of any fat or sinew. Cut the meat into 1 cm (½ inch) slices. Cut each slice into 1 cm (½ inch) strips about 7.5 cm (3 inches) long.

Cut strips of equal size so they cook evenly

2 Wipe the mushroom caps with a damp paper towel and trim the stalks even with the caps. Set the mushrooms stalk-side down on the chopping board and slice them.

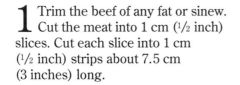

3 Peel the onions and cut a thin slice from one side of each so that the onion sits flat on the chopping board. Cut the onions into slices of medium thickness. Strip the tarragon leaves from the stalks and chop the leaves.

2 COOK THE SAUTE

Juice is sealed in as meat strips brown over high heat

1 Heat half of the butter and oil in the sauté pan until starting to brown. Add half of the beef strips, sprinkle with a little salt and pepper, and cook over very high heat, stirring, until the meat is well browned but still rare in the centre, 2-3 minutes. Remove the meat with the slotted spoon and add more butter if the pan is dry. Brown the remaining beef in the same way, then remove it and set aside.

Stir in flour until
it is absorbed by
mushrooms

2 Heat the remaining butter and oil
in the sauté pan, add the onions,
separating the slices into rings, and
sauté over medium heat until softened
and browned, stirring occasionally,
5-7 minutes. Transfer them to a bowl
with the slotted spoon.

3 Add the mushrooms
to the pan and sauté
until all the moisture has
evaporated, 4-5 minutes.
Stirring constantly, add the
flour and cook 1 minute.

4 Pour in the stock and bring
to a boil, stirring so the
sauce thickens smoothly.

Stock combines
with flour to
make rich sauce

5 Return the onions to the pan, add
salt and pepper, and simmer
2 minutes. Stir in the mustard and
heat gently without boiling.

! TAKE CARE !
*If the mustard boils, the sauce will
be bitter.*

6 Return the beef and its juices to the sauté pan and heat gently but thoroughly, 2-3 minutes. If the beef is overcooked, it will be tough.

Tangy soured cream is favourite Russian flavouring

7 Stir in the soured cream and heat the sauté about 1 minute longer. Taste for seasoning.

ANNE SAYS
"Do not let the mixture get too hot or the soured cream may curdle."

 TO SERVE
Serve immediately with cooked fresh noodles. Sprinkle with the chopped tarragon.

Fresh noodles are an excellent accompaniment

Beef strips are lightly sautéed so they are still rare in centre

---

V A R I A T I O N

BEEF SAUTE WITH PARIKA

Here paprika is added with red peppers for a colourful version of Russian Beef Sauté.

1 Trim and cut the fillet as directed in the main recipe.
2 Prepare the onions as directed; omit the mushrooms and the mustard.
3 With a sharp movement, twist the cores out of 2 red peppers, then halve the peppers and scrape out the seeds. Cut away the white ribs on the inside. Set each pepper half cut-side down on a board, flatten it with the heel of your hand, and slice it lengthwise into strips.
4 Sprinkle the beef strips with about 30 ml (2 tbsp) paprika and toss them until they are well coated. Fry the beef strips in butter and oil in a sauté pan over medium-high heat, taking care not to scorch the paprika.
5 Fry the onions as directed in the main recipe and remove.
6 Sauté the red peppers until tender, 5-7 minutes. Sprinkle over the flour, make the sauce, finish and serve as directed.

VEAL ESCALOPES WITH SAGE AND PARMA HAM

Saltimbocca

🍽 SERVES 4   🥣 WORK TIME 20-25 MINUTES   ♨ COOKING TIME 10-12 MINUTES

EQUIPMENT

chef's knife

palette knife

rolling pin

parchment paper*

large frying pan

wooden spoon

chopping board   plate

* greaseproof paper can also be used

Made from veal escalopes, the most popular of all veal cuts, saltimbocca means literally "jump in the mouth". The meat is flattened to make the thinnest of tender, delicate slices, which are topped with aromatic sage leaves and paper-thin slices of Parma ham, then quickly sautéed in butter. The pan juices are deglazed with white wine for a simple sauce. The dish is best served with small pasta quills or shells.

GETTING AHEAD

Saltimbocca can be prepared up to the end of step 6 up to 8 hours ahead and kept covered in the refrigerator. Do not overlap the saltimbocca, but layer them between sheets of parchment or greaseproof paper so that they do not stick together. The veal should be cooked just before serving.

INGREDIENTS

veal escalopes

Parma ham

white wine

butter

fresh sage leaves

ANNE SAYS
"*Parma ham (prosciutto di Parma) is a salt-cured, air-dried raw ham, which is always very thinly sliced. You can find it in large supermarkets and specialist food shops.*"

ORDER OF WORK

1 PREPARE THE SALTIMBOCCA

2 COOK THE SALTIMBOCCA

metric	SHOPPING LIST	imperial
4	veal escalopes, total weight about 500 g (1 lb)	4
4	thin slices of Parma or cooked ham, total weight 75 g (2 ½ oz)	4
12	fresh sage leaves, more for garnish	12
60 g	butter	2 oz
75 ml	white wine	2 ½ fl oz
	salt and pepper	

1 PREPARE THE SALTIMBOCCA

Flatten veal gently with rolling pin so fibres of meat are not broken

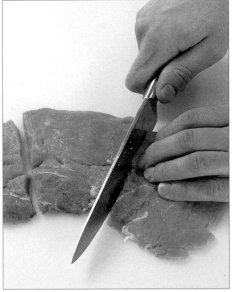

1 Put a veal escalope between 2 sheets of parchment paper. Pound it to a thickness of about 3 mm (⅛ inch) with the rolling pin.

2 Peel the parchment paper away from the meat. With the chef's knife, cut the pounded veal escalopes into 3 pieces.

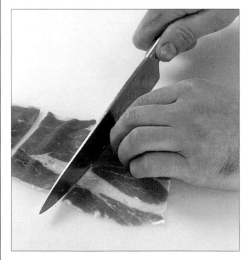

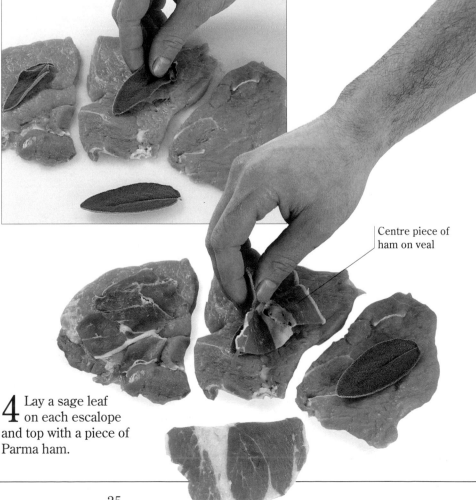

Centre piece of ham on veal

3 Trim away any rind and excess fat from 1 of the Parma ham slices. Cut the slice of ham into 3 pieces.

ANNE SAYS
"The veal shrinks during cooking so the pieces of Parma ham should be a little smaller than the escalopes."

4 Lay a sage leaf on each escalope and top with a piece of Parma ham.

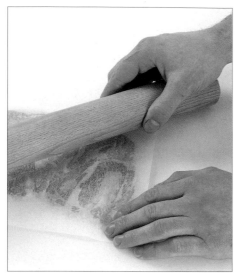

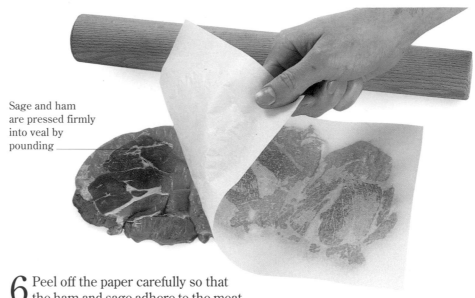

Sage and ham
are pressed firmly
into veal by
pounding

5 Put a piece of parchment paper over the veal and ham pieces, and pound gently to press the ham onto the meat.

6 Peel off the paper carefully so that the ham and sage adhere to the meat. Prepare the remaining escalopes, sage leaves, and ham slices in the same way.

2 COOK THE SALTIMBOCCA

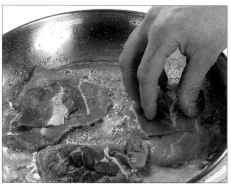

1 Heat the butter in the frying pan. Add a few of the saltimbocca to the pan and brown over medium heat, about 2 minutes.

! TAKE CARE !
Veal escalopes cook very quickly and will be tough if overcooked.

Brown veal lightly
so it remains tender

Browned juices
left in pan are
basis for sauce

2 Turn each saltimbocca with the palette knife and brown the other side, 1-2 minutes.

3 As the saltimbocca are cooked, transfer them to the plate and keep them warm.

4 Add the white wine to the pan and heat to boiling, stirring to dissolve the pan juices. Season to taste.

ANNE SAYS

"*Salt may not be needed because the Parma ham is salty.*"

Stir up pan juices so they dissolve in wine

Sauce made from cooking juices gives veal a glaze

🍴 **TO SERVE**

Transfer the saltimbocca to a warmed platter or individual plates using the palette knife. Spoon the sauce around the veal and garnish with sage leaves.

Fresh sage leaf garnish echoes flavouring in saltimbocca

VARIATION

VEAL PICCATE WITH MUSHROOMS AND MARSALA

Another favourite veal recipe – these small fried escalopes are served in a rich mushroom sauce

1 Wipe the caps of 250 g (8 oz) mushrooms with a damp paper towel and trim the stalks level with the caps. Set the mushroom caps stalk-side down on a chopping board and slice.

2 Set the flat side of a chef's knife on top of 2 garlic cloves and strike it with your fist. Discard the skin and finely chop the garlic.

3 Flatten the veal escalopes as directed and cut each into 5-6 pieces. Omit the Parma ham and sage.

4 Coat the pieces of veal lightly in 30 g (1 oz) plain flour, seasoned with salt and pepper, discarding the excess.

5 Fry the veal in 30-45 g (1-1½ oz) butter until browned, 1-2 minutes on each side, cooking them in several batches. Transfer them to a plate.

6 Heat 30 g (1 oz) butter in the pan, add the mushrooms, garlic, salt, and pepper, and cook, stirring occasionally, 2-3 minutes. Stir in 45-60 ml (3-4 tbsp) double cream and simmer 2 minutes.

7 Add 60 ml (4 tbsp) Marsala, Madeira, or sweet sherry and cook 1 minute longer.

8 Return the veal escalopes to the sauce, heat gently 1 minute, and serve. Pasta is an excellent accompaniment.

PORK AND GINGER SUKIYAKI

 SERVES 6   WORK TIME 15-20 MINUTES*   COOKING TIME 15-20 MINUTES

EQUIPMENT

chef's knife

small knife

sieve

bowls

wooden spoon

slotted spoon

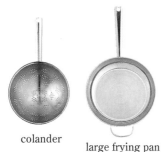
colander

large frying pan

chopping board

Sukiyaki, traditionally prepared with beef and cooked directly at the table, does not have a long history in Japan. It was among preparations introduced by beef-eating western diplomats and merchants. Here innovation goes a step further: very thin slices of pork are half stir-fried and half simmered in saké and soy sauce.

GETTING AHEAD

Pork and Ginger Sukiyaki is best prepared and cooked just before serving.

*plus 1-2 hours marinating time

metric	SHOPPING LIST	imperial
1 kg	pork tenderloins	2 lb
2.5 cm	piece of fresh root ginger	1 inch
125 ml	saké	4 fl oz
60 ml	soy sauce	4 tbsp
15 ml	sweet sherry	1 tbsp
5 ml	granulated sugar	1 tsp
60 g	dried oriental mushrooms	2 oz
10	spring onions	10
75 ml	vegetable oil, more if needed	2½ fl oz
	cellophane noodles for serving (optional)	

INGREDIENTS

pork tenderloins

granulated sugar

dried oriental mushrooms

spring onions

saké

soy sauce

vegetable oil

sweet sherry

fresh root ginger

ANNE SAYS
"Sherry and sugar stand in for the sweet Japanese rice wine, mirin. You can use mirin if you prefer; it is available from Japanese and other oriental supermarkets."

ORDER OF WORK

1 **PREPARE AND MARINATE THE PORK**

2 **PREPARE THE REMAINING INGREDIENTS**

3 **COOK THE SUKIYAKI**

1 PREPARE AND MARINATE THE PORK

Thin, uniform slices ensure that meat cooks quickly and evenly

Be sure knife is sharp for easy slicing

1 Using the chef's knife, trim the pork tenderloins of any fat and membrane. With the same knife, cut diagonally across each pork tenderloin to make thin, even slices.

2 Coarsely chop the ginger (see box, below). Combine the ginger, saké, soy sauce, sweet sherry, and sugar in a non-metallic bowl.

3 Add the pork slices to the bowl and stir so all the slices are coated with the marinade. Cover and marinate 1-2 hours in the refrigerator. While the pork is marinating, prepare the remaining ingredients.

HOW TO PEEL AND CHOP FRESH ROOT GINGER

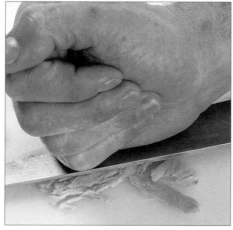

1 With a small knife, peel the skin from the root ginger. Using a chef's knife, slice the ginger, cutting across the fibrous grain.

2 Place the flat side of the chef's knife on the slices of root ginger and crush them by pressing firmly on the blade with your fist.

3 Chop the slices of root ginger coarsely or finely, according to recipe requirements.

2 PREPARE THE REMAINING INGREDIENTS

1 Put the dried mushrooms in a bowl and cover with warm water. Soak the mushrooms until plump, about 30 minutes, then drain them well in the colander.

Tip mushrooms into colander to drain

2 Trim the roots and tops of the spring onions. Cut the onions diagonally into 4 cm (1½ inch) pieces.

3 COOK THE SUKIYAKI

1 Heat 15 ml (1 tbsp) oil in the frying pan. Add the mushrooms and spring onions and sauté over medium heat, stirring often, until they soften, 2-3 minutes. Transfer to a large bowl. Drain the pork in the sieve, reserving the liquid.

2 Heat another tablespoon of oil in the pan. Add one-quarter of the pork and sauté over very high heat, stirring constantly, until the meat is lightly coloured, 2-3 minutes.

3 Transfer the cooked pork to the bowl containing the mushrooms and spring onions. Cook the remaining pork in batches, adding more oil to the pan as needed.

4 Pour the reserved marinade into the pan. Return the mushrooms, spring onions, and pork to the pan.

Reserved marinade adds flavour

Spring onions add vivid green colour

5 Simmer the mixture in the marinade until the meat is just heated through, 1-2 minutes.

! TAKE CARE !
Do not overcook the pork or it will be tough.

Stir meat and vegetables so they are heated evenly

TO SERVE
Taste and season with more saké, soy sauce, sherry, and sugar, if needed. Transfer the sukiyaki to warmed individual plates. If you like, serve in nests of cellophane noodles.

Tender pork slices are flavoured with ginger, saké, and soy sauce

Nest of cellophane noodles forms a delicate background

BEEF, GINGER, AND SESAME SUKIYAKI

Here, beef is combined with fresh root ginger, shiitake mushrooms, and sesame seeds, plus sesame oil for fragrance.

1 Trim the fat and sinew from 1 kg (2 lb) braising steak, then slice the beef as directed for the pork.
2 Prepare the ginger and make the marinade as directed, then let the beef marinate, 1-2 hours.
3 Wipe 250 g (8 oz) fresh shiitake mushrooms with a damp paper towel and trim the stalks. Cut the mushrooms into 1 cm (1/2 inch) slices. Alternatively, soak 45 g (1 1/2 oz) dried shiitake mushrooms in a bowl of warm water until they are plump, about 30 minutes. Drain and continue as for fresh mushrooms.
4 Prepare the spring onions as directed in the main recipe.
5 Toast 30 ml (2 tbsp) sesame seeds: heat a small frying pan over medium heat, add the seeds, and toast, stirring occasionally, until lightly browned, 2-3 minutes.
6 Cook the sukiyaki as directed in the main recipe, stirring in 5-10 ml (1-2 tsp) sesame oil at the end of cooking.
7 Serve immediately on a bed of boiled Japanese noodles, such as udon or soba, arranging the slices of beef, spring onions, and shiitake mushrooms decoratively; sprinkle with the toasted sesame seeds.

RACK OF LAMB WITH SAUTEED CUCUMBERS AND MINT

🍴 SERVES 4   🥣 WORK TIME 35-40 MINUTES   ☕ ROASTING TIME 25-30 MINUTES

EQUIPMENT

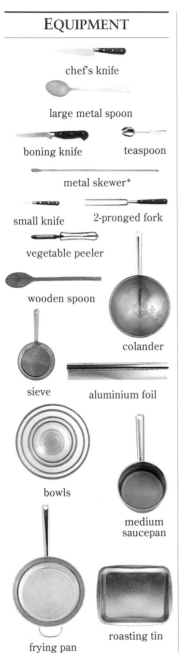

chef's knife

large metal spoon

boning knife   teaspoon

metal skewer*

small knife   2-pronged fork

vegetable peeler

wooden spoon

colander

sieve   aluminium foil

bowls

medium saucepan

frying pan   roasting tin

chopping board

* meat thermometer can also be used

Lightly sautéed cucumber adds a crisp, refreshing touch to the traditional combination of roast lamb with mint. When choosing rack of lamb, look for a small joint with white fat and a good pink colour in the lean. Be sure the butcher trims off the chine bone (backbone) that joins the rib bones together.

GETTING AHEAD

The lamb can be prepared up to 1 day ahead and kept, covered, in the refrigerator. Roast the lamb and cook the cucumbers just before serving.

metric	SHOPPING LIST	imperial
2	racks of lamb (best ends of neck), weighing 750 g-1 kg (1½-2 lb) each, chine bones removed	2
2	garlic cloves	2
30 ml	olive oil	2 tbsp
	salt and pepper	
	For the sautéed cucumbers	
2	cucumbers	2
8-10	sprigs of fresh mint	8-10
30 g	butter	1 oz
	For the gravy	
125 ml	white wine	4 fl oz
250 ml	beef or brown veal stock (see box, page 36)	8 fl oz

INGREDIENTS

racks of lamb

cucumbers

fresh mint

butter

olive oil

garlic cloves

white wine

beef stock

ORDER OF WORK

1 PREPARE THE RACKS OF LAMB

2 ROAST THE LAMB

3 PREPARE AND SAUTE THE CUCUMBERS

4 MAKE THE MINT GRAVY

1 PREPARE THE RACKS OF LAMB

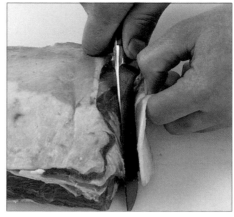

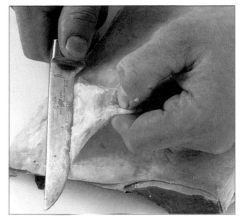

1 Set a rack of lamb on the chopping board, ribs upwards, and, with the boning knife, cut out any sinew lying under the ribs.

2 Turn the rack over. Cut away the small crescent of cartilage at one end of the rack.

3 Make a small incision under the thin layer of skin covering the fat. Using your fingers, pull off the skin.

ANNE SAYS
"If you can't get a good grip, use a clean tea towel to help."

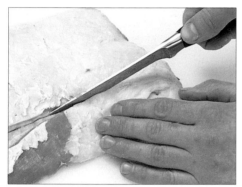

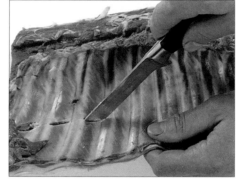

4 Score through the fat and meat down to the rib bones, about 5 cm (2 inches) from the ends of the bones.

5 Turn the rack over. Place it over the edge of the board and score down to the bone about 5 cm (2 inches) from the ends of the bones.

Thin layer of fat will keep meat moist during roasting

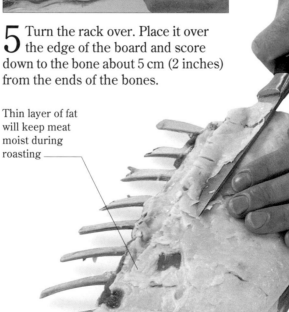

6 Cut out the meat between the bones, using the point of the boning knife. Scrape the bones clean.

! TAKE CARE !
Be sure to scrape away all skin or it will spoil the appearance of the roasted rack.

7 Turn the rack over and cut away the thin layer of meat and most of the fat, if necessary. Repeat the process for the second rack.

ANNE SAYS
"To save time you may prefer to ask your butcher to prepare the racks."

2 ROAST THE LAMB

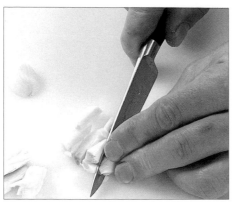

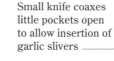

Small knife coaxes little pockets open to allow insertion of garlic slivers

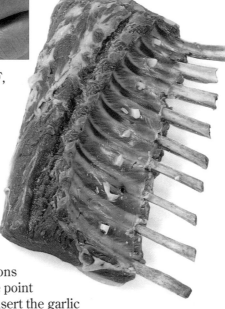

1 Heat the oven to 230°C (450°F, Gas 8). Peel the garlic cloves with your fingers, then cut each one lengthwise into 4-5 thin slivers using the chef's knife.

2 Make several incisions in the lamb with the point of the small knife and insert the garlic slivers in the little pockets, pushing them in with the point of the knife.

Slivers of garlic add piquant flavour

3 Transfer the racks to the roasting tin, laying them ribs downwards. Wrap the scraped bones in foil to prevent them from being burned. Spoon the oil over the lamb and sprinkle with salt and pepper.

4 Roast the lamb in the heated oven 25-30 minutes, basting the racks once or twice with the juices in the roasting tin. The meat will shrink away from the bones a little during roasting. Meanwhile, prepare and sauté the cucumbers.

5 Test the lamb with the skewer: when inserted for 30 seconds it will feel warm to the touch when withdrawn. A meat thermometer should register 60°C (140°F).

ANNE SAYS
"Timings and temperatures here are for medium-done. If you prefer your lamb better done, roast it another 5 minutes."

3 PREPARE AND SAUTE THE CUCUMBERS

1 Peel and trim the cucumbers and cut them lengthwise in half. Scoop out the seeds with the teaspoon.

Spoon removes seeds neatly

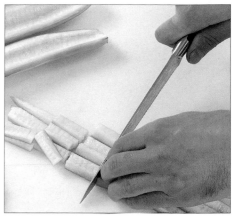

2 Cut the halves lengthwise into 3-4 strips, then gather the strips into a bundle and cut them crosswise into 4 cm (1¹/₂ inch) sticks.

3 Strip the mint leaves from the stalks, reserving a few sprigs for garnish. Set the stalks aside for the gravy. Pile the leaves on the chopping board and chop them finely.

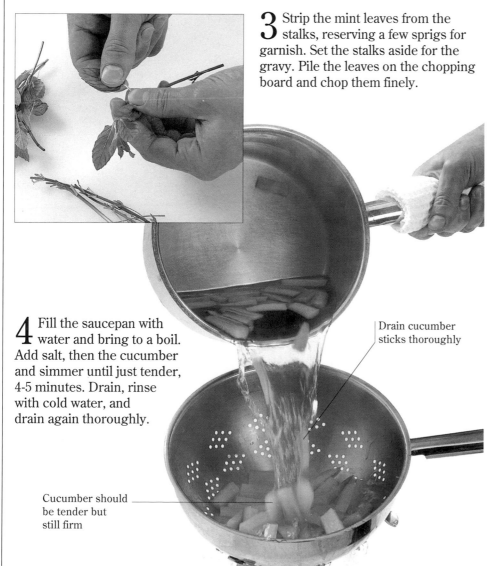

4 Fill the saucepan with water and bring to a boil. Add salt, then the cucumber and simmer until just tender, 4-5 minutes. Drain, rinse with cold water, and drain again thoroughly.

Drain cucumber sticks thoroughly

Cucumber should be tender but still firm

5 Heat the butter in the frying pan. Add the cucumber sticks and sauté over low heat, stirring and shaking the pan, until heated through, 1-2 minutes. Stir in the chopped mint and season with salt and pepper.

! TAKE CARE !
Do not overcook the cucumber or it will be bitter.

HOW TO MAKE BEEF OR BROWN VEAL STOCK

Stock is based on raw meat bones gently simmered with aromatic vegetables in water. Ask your butcher to cut the bones into pieces. Boiling should be avoided because it makes the stock cloudy. Season the stock mildly so that it does not overpower dishes to which it is added. For light coloured and delicately flavoured dishes, use White Veal Stock, which is made using bones that have not been browned.

White Veal Stock

Put 4-5 veal bones, cut in pieces, in a large stockpot, add water to cover, and bring to a boil. Simmer 5 minutes, then drain the bones and rinse well under cold water. Return the bones to the pot, and add 2 onions and 2 carrots, peeled and quartered, 2 quartered celery sticks, a bouquet garni, 10 black peppercorns, 1 garlic clove, and water to cover. Continue as for the brown veal or beef stock below.

🍽 MAKES 2-3 LITRES/3½-5 PINTS

🥄 WORK TIME 20-30 MINUTES

🍲 COOKING TIME 4-5 HOURS

SHOPPING LIST

1.8-2.3 kg	beef or veal bones, cut in pieces	4-5 lb
2	onions	2
2	carrots	2
2	celery sticks	2
4 litres	water, more if needed	7 pints
1	large bouquet garni	1
10	black peppercorns	10
1	garlic clove	1
15 ml	tomato purée	1 tbsp

Add vegetables to well-browned bones

2 Peel and quarter the onions and carrots. Quarter the celery. Add the vegetables to the tin and brown, 15-20 minutes, stirring occasionally.

ANNE SAYS

"Thorough browning of the bones and vegetables gives the stock flavour and colour."

1 Heat the oven to 230°C (450°F, Gas 8). Put the bones in a large roasting tin; roast until well browned, 30-40 minutes, stirring occasionally.

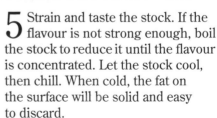

3 Transfer the bones and vegetables to a stockpot with a slotted spoon. Discard the fat from the roasting tin and add 500 ml (16 fl oz) of the water. Bring to a boil, stirring to dissolve the juices in the roasting tin.

4 Add the liquid to the stockpot with the remaining ingredients and enough water just to cover the bones. Bring slowly to a boil, skimming often, then simmer gently, uncovered, 4-5 hours, skimming occasionally. Add water if the stock evaporates.

5 Strain and taste the stock. If the flavour is not strong enough, boil the stock to reduce it until the flavour is concentrated. Let the stock cool, then chill. When cold, the fat on the surface will be solid and easy to discard.

4 MAKE THE MINT GRAVY

1 When the lamb is cooked to your taste, transfer the racks to the chopping board. Discard the foil used to cover the bone tips. Cover the racks with foil and set aside.

Foil will keep lamb warm while you make gravy

2 Discard the fat from the roasting tin. Add the wine to the tin and boil until reduced by half, stirring to dissolve the roasting juices. Add the reserved mint stalks and the stock; boil until well flavoured, 5-7 minutes. Season to taste. Strain and keep warm.

🍽 **TO SERVE** Carve the racks of lamb by cutting down between each rib bone. Arrange the chops on a warmed serving platter and surround with the cucumber. Garnish with the reserved mint sprigs. Serve the mint gravy separately.

Lamb chops arranged this way look spectacular

V A R I A T I O N

RACK OF LAMB COATED WITH PARSLEY AND BREADCRUMBS

Here roast racks of lamb are given a crisp finish with parsley and breadcrumbs. Serve with vegetables, such as carrots and okra, glazed with butter.

1 Prepare and roast the racks of lamb as directed in the main recipe.

2 Omit the cucumbers and mint.

3 Trim the crusts from 4 slices of white bread. Work the slices in a food processor or blender to form crumbs.

4 Chop the sprigs from a small bunch of parsley.

5 Melt 45 g (1 1/2 oz) butter in a frying pan, add the breadcrumbs, and cook, stirring, until just golden, 2-3 minutes. Stir in the chopped parsley and season with salt and pepper.

6 Heat the grill. When the lamb is cooked to your taste, press the breadcrumb mixture onto the surface and baste with the roasting juices. Grill until lightly browned, 1-2 minutes.

7 Arrange the racks in a guard of honour, if you like, and make the gravy as directed, omitting the mint. Serve with vegetables and a herb decoration.

MINUTE STEAK
MARCHAND DE VIN

🍽 SERVES 4   🥣 WORK TIME 15-20 MINUTES   🍲 COOKING TIME 40-50 MINUTES

EQUIPMENT

heavy-based
frying pan

plate   tongs

small baking dishes

large metal spoon

wooden spoon

chef's knife

aluminium foil

chopping board

ANNE SAYS
*"A cast-iron frying pan is
the best to use because it
distributes the heat evenly."*

*In this simplest of all steak recipes, thin
"minute" steaks are cut from a piece of beef
fillet and pan-fried. Shallots are sautéed in
the pan, which is then deglazed with red wine
for a simple sauce. When roasted, garlic and
shallots become surprisingly mild and are the
ideal accompaniment, although they can be
omitted to save time. Choose a good red
wine for cooking that you will also want
to drink with the meal.*

GETTING AHEAD
The garlic and shallots should be roasted and the steaks
fried just before serving.

metric	SHOPPING LIST	imperial
1	large bulb of garlic	1
	vegetable oil, for baking and frying	
	salt and pepper	
10	small shallots	10
1	small bunch of parsley	1
2-3	sprigs of fresh thyme	2-3
750 g	piece of fillet of beef	1½ lb
250 ml	red wine	8 fl oz
30 g	butter	1 oz

INGREDIENTS

fillet of beef

shallots

vegetable oil

butter   parsley

head of garlic

red wine

fresh thyme

ORDER OF WORK

1 ROAST THE GARLIC
AND SHALLOTS

2 PREPARE THE
INGREDIENTS FOR
THE SAUCE AND
FRY THE STEAKS

3 FINISH THE DISH

1 ROAST THE GARLIC AND SHALLOTS

1 Heat the oven to 170° C (325° F, Gas 3). To separate the garlic cloves, crush the bulb using your hands to exert pressure. Break the garlic cloves apart, discarding the root.

Pressure from hands separates garlic cloves easily

2 Put the garlic cloves in one of the baking dishes, add 15 ml (1 tbsp) oil, and sprinkle with salt and pepper. Stir until they are evenly coated.

3 Trim the roots and remove any papery or loose skin from the shallots, without peeling them. Put the shallots in the second baking dish, setting aside 2 for the sauce. Toss them with 30 ml (2 tbsp) oil, salt, and pepper.

4 Transfer the garlic cloves and shallots to the heated oven. Roast the garlic 30-35 minutes and the shallots 25-30 minutes until tender.

Oil-tossed shallots and garlic cloves roasted in skin are glossy and tender

HOW TO CHOP A SHALLOT

For a standard chop, make slices that are about 3 mm ($^1/_8$ inch) thick. For a fine chop, slice the shallot as thinly as possible.

1 Peel the outer, papery skin from the shallot. If necessary, separate the shallot into sections at the root and peel the sections. Set flat-side down on a chopping board. Hold the shallot steady with your fingers and slice horizontally, leaving the slices attached at the root.

2 Slice vertically through the shallot, again leaving the root end uncut.

3 Cut across the shallot to make fine dice. Continue chopping the shallot if necessary until it is very fine.

2 PREPARE THE INGREDIENTS FOR THE SAUCE AND FRY THE STEAKS

1 Strip the parsley leaves from the stalks and pile them on the chopping board. With the chef's knife, finely chop the leaves. Peel and finely chop the reserved shallots (see box, page 39). Strip the thyme leaves from the stalks.

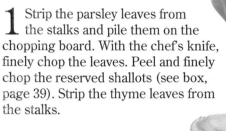

Set shallot flat-side down on work surface before starting to chop

2 Trim any fat from the beef fillet and cut it into 1 cm (¹/₂ inch) steaks, cutting the steaks slightly thicker at the narrow end of the fillet. You should have 8 steaks.

3 Pound the thicker steaks with the flat of the chef's knife so that they resemble the larger steaks. Put the steaks on the plate and sprinkle both sides with salt and pepper.

4 Heat about 15 ml (1 tbsp) oil in the frying pan. Fry 4 steaks over moderately high heat until well browned on 1 side, 1-2 minutes. Turn them with the tongs; continue frying until well browned but still pink in the centre, 1-2 minutes longer.

Pressing with your finger is best test for completion of cooking

5 The steaks are done when they yield if pressed with your finger. If firm, they are well-done. Transfer the steaks to a plate, cover with foil to keep warm, and fry the remaining 4 steaks, adding another 15 ml (1 tbsp) of oil to the pan. Transfer them to the plate, cover, and keep warm.

3 FINISH THE DISH

1 Add the chopped shallots to the pan and sauté, stirring, until soft but not brown, 1-2 minutes. Add the red wine and thyme and bring to a boil, stirring. Boil to slightly thicken and concentrate the flavour, 3-5 minutes.

Add parsley to sauce at end of cooking so it retains colour and aroma

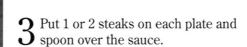

2 Stir in most of the parsley and taste for seasoning. Add the butter and swirl the sauce, taking the pan on and off the heat, so that the butter thickens the sauce without melting to oil.

3 Put 1 or 2 steaks on each plate and spoon over the sauce.

🍽 TO SERVE

Sprinkle the steaks with the remaining parsley and chopped salad leaves, if you like. Arrange the garlic and shallots around the steaks for diners to peel; serve with French fries.

Steak is plump, tender, and juicy

V A R I A T I O N

MINUTE STEAK DIJONNAISE

In this simple variation, red wine is replaced with white wine, and tangy Dijon mustard and cream are added to the sauce. Instead of roasted garlic and shallots, the steaks are accompanied by caramelized pickling onions.

1 Omit the roasted shallots and garlic. Put 20-24 pickling onions in a bowl, cover with hot water, and let stand 2 minutes. Drain the onions and peel them with a small knife, leaving a little of the root to hold the onion together. Roast the onions as for the shallots, sprinkling them with 15 ml (1 tbsp) sugar halfway through cooking.

2 Chop 2 shallots. Prepare and fry the steaks as directed.

3 Stir 250 ml (8 fl oz) dry white wine into the pan and boil until reduced by half, 2-3 minutes. Take the pan from the heat and stir in 15 ml (1 tbsp) Dijon mustard and 30-45 ml (2-3 tbsp) double cream, omitting the butter. Taste for seasoning.

4 Put 1 or 2 steaks on each plate. Coat the steaks with the sauce, set the onions on the side, decorated with parsley sprigs, and serve with homemade game chips (see page 124).

BUTTERFLIED LEG OF LAMB

🍴 SERVES 6-8   🥄 WORK TIME 35-40 MINUTES*   ♨ GRILLING TIME 20-30 MINUTES

EQUIPMENT

bowls

boning knife

chef's knife

pastry brush

wooden spoon

metal skewer

2-pronged fork

carving knife

chopping board

INGREDIENTS

leg of lamb

garlic cloves

fresh rosemary

olive oil

red wine

fresh thyme

Butterflying a leg of lamb is quite simple: the bone is removed and the meat is slit so that it lies flat, and can be grilled in about a quarter of the time that a whole leg takes to roast. The marinade of just oil, garlic, and herbs is delicious, whether the lamb is cooked under the grill or outdoors on the barbecue. Warm new potatoes tossed with a herb vinaigrette are the perfect accompaniment.

GETTING AHEAD

The lamb can be butterflied and marinated up to 4 hours ahead. It is best grilled just before serving. To serve cold, cook the lamb only until rare and let it cool before slicing.

* plus 1-4 hours marinating time

ANNE SAYS

"If your grill is not very hot, brown the lamb first on both sides in a frying pan on top of the stove, then grill 7-10 minutes on each side."

ORDER OF WORK

1 BONE AND BUTTERFLY THE LEG OF LAMB

2 MARINATE AND GRILL THE LAMB; MAKE THE SAUCE

metric	SHOPPING LIST	imperial
1	leg of lamb, weighing about 2.2 kg (5 lb)	1
4	garlic cloves	4
3-4	sprigs of fresh rosemary	3-4
3-4	sprigs of fresh thyme	3-4
30 ml	olive oil, more for grill rack	2 tbsp
	salt and pepper	
45 ml	red wine	3 tbsp

1 BONE AND BUTTERFLY THE LEG OF LAMB

1 Using the boning knife, trim off the skin and all but a thin layer of fat from the lamb. With the pelvic bone upwards and using the boning knife, outline the edges of the bones that are exposed.

2 Cut deeper around the pelvic bone, freeing it at the joint and cutting through the tendons connecting it to the leg bone. Remove the pelvic bone. Grasp the tip of the shank (lower-leg) bone and cut all tendons at the base of the bone.

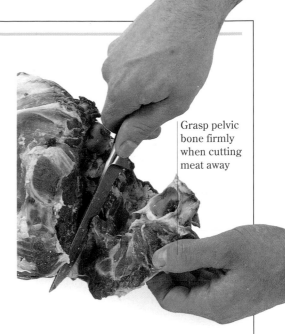

Grasp pelvic bone firmly when cutting meat away

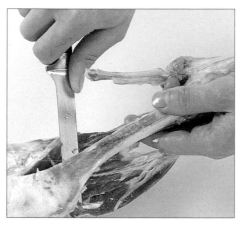

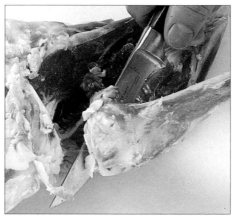

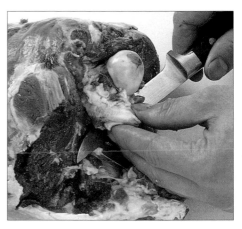

3 Cut the meat away from the shank bone, keeping the meat in one piece. When the bone is clean, locate the knee joint at the point where the shank bone is connected to the leg bone, and scrape away meat and fat to expose the joint.

4 Cut the tendons at the joint and remove the shank bone.

5 With the knife, gently release each end of the leg bone from the meat.

6 Cut and scrape to clean the leg bone, easing it out as you work. Twist the bone and pull it out.

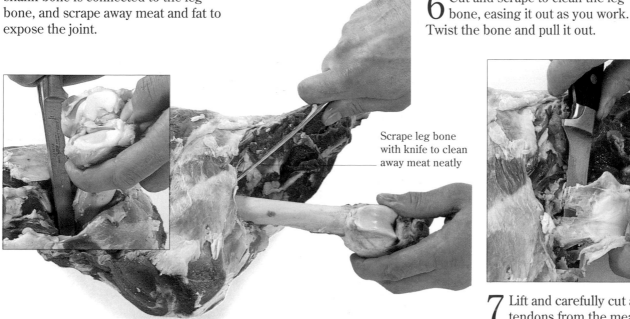

Scrape leg bone with knife to clean away meat neatly

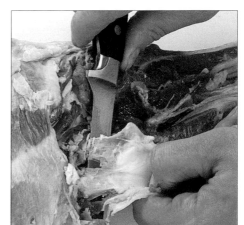

7 Lift and carefully cut away the tendons from the meat.

8 Insert the blade of the chef's knife into the cavity left by the leg bone. Holding the blade horizontal, cut outwards to slit open one side.

Open out boned lamb

9 Lift up the flap created by cutting open one side, and spread out the meat into a "butterfly" shape.

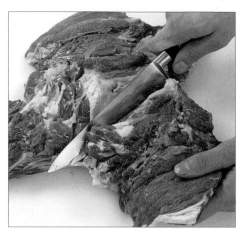

10 Working from the centre, make a cut in the thick muscle so the leg can be opened out flat.

MARINATE AND GRILL THE LAMB; MAKE THE SAUCE

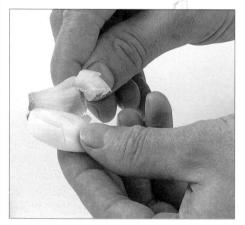

1 Set the flat side of the chef's knife on top of each garlic clove and strike it. Discard the skin and finely chop the garlic. Strip the rosemary and thyme leaves from the stalks and chop.

2 Brush the grill rack and both sides of the lamb with oil. Rub half of the garlic and herbs into the top. Marinate 1 hour at room temperature, or up to 4 hours in the refrigerator.

3 Heat the grill to high. Sprinkle the lamb with salt and pepper and grill 7.5 cm (3 inches) from the heat until brown and slightly charred, 10-15 minutes. Turn the lamb over.

4 Sprinkle the lamb with the remaining garlic, herbs, salt, and pepper, and continue grilling until the skewer inserted in the thickest part of the meat for 30 seconds is warm to the touch when withdrawn, 10-15 minutes. Remove the lamb from the rack, cover loosely with foil, and let it rest in a warm place 5 minutes; reserve the juices in the pan.

Meat will be cooked pink if warm inside when tested with skewer

5 Add the red wine to the grill pan and heat on top of the stove, stirring to dissolve the pan juices.

Carve meat on diagonal for larger slices

6 Cut the lamb in thick diagonal slices.

TO SERVE
Divide the slices between individual plates and spoon the sauce over the meat. Serve with new potatoes.

Warm new potatoes are dressed with herb vinaigrette

BUTTERFLIED LOIN OF PORK

Like leg of lamb, loin of pork is a good meat to butterfly. Dijon mustard is added to the garlic and herbs to permeate the pork with more flavour and become the basis for the sauce.

1 Butterfly a 1.4 kg (3 lb) boneless loin of pork: unroll the flap of meat left from boning and set the pork on a chopping board, fat-side down. With a chef's knife make a horizontal slit in the meat, cutting almost through to the other side. Open it out like a book.
2 Press the loin into a flat rectangle and cover with parchment paper. Pound it with a rolling pin to tenderize it and achieve an even thickness.
3 Brush the pork with Dijon mustard, using about 30 ml (2 tbsp) per side. Sprinkle with double the quantity of oil. Prepare double quantities of chopped garlic and herbs, then rub half into the top of the pork; marinate as directed.
4 Grill the pork 13 cm (5 inches) from the heat, 12-15 minutes. Turn and sprinkle with the remaining garlic and herbs. Grill until a skewer inserted in the thickest part for 30 seconds is hot to the touch, 12-15 minutes longer.
5 Make the sauce as directed, replacing the red wine with white and adding 10 ml (2 tsp) Dijon mustard.
6 Arrange slices on a platter and accompany with the sauce, and with mixed salad leaves, if you like.

LAMB CHOPS IN PAPER CASES WITH FENNEL

🍽 SERVES 4   🥣 WORK TIME 25-30 MINUTES   ♨ COOKING TIME 35-40 MINUTES

EQUIPMENT

bowls

small knife

chef's knife

2 large frying pans

pastry brush

kitchen scissors

fork

metal spoon

medium saucepan

plate

slotted spoon

palette knife

pencil

wooden spoon

teaspoon

chopping board

baking sheet

parchment paper

Cooking in a paper case is widely popular, and with good reason. Meats enclosed in parchment steam in their own juices with minimum fat and maximum flavour. Here lamb chops are first browned, then baked in paper on a bed of fennel and tomatoes with a splash of aniseed liqueur to enhance the flavour. The paper parcels puff up golden brown in the oven and make an attractive presentation for each diner to open.

GETTING AHEAD

The lamb chop parcels can be prepared up to 2 hours in advance and refrigerated. Bake them just before serving.

metric	SHOPPING LIST	imperial
750 g	tomatoes	1¹/₂ lb
1 kg	fennel bulbs	2 lb
2	garlic cloves	2
60 ml	olive oil	4 tbsp
45 ml	pastis	3 tbsp
	salt and pepper	
4	lamb loin chops, each 2.5 cm (1 inch) thick, total weight about 625 g (1¹/₄ lb)	4
	melted butter for brushing	
	For the egg glaze	
1	egg	1
2.5 ml	salt	¹/₂ tsp

INGREDIENTS

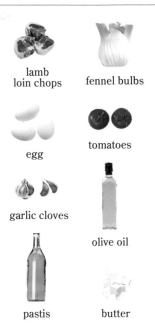

lamb loin chops

fennel bulbs

egg

tomatoes

garlic cloves

olive oil

pastis

butter

ANNE SAYS
"Pastis, the French aniseed- and liquorice-flavoured liqueur, complements the taste of fennel; however, any aniseed-flavoured liqueur, such as Pernod, can be substituted."

ORDER OF WORK

1 PREPARE THE VEGETABLES AND LAMB CHOPS

2 MAKE THE PAPER CASES

3 FILL THE PAPER CASES AND BAKE

1 PREPARE THE VEGETABLES AND LAMB CHOPS

1 Cut the cores from the tomatoes and score an "x" on the base of each with the tip of the small knife. Immerse them in a pan of boiling water until the skin starts to split, 8-15 seconds depending on their ripeness. Using the slotted spoon, transfer at once to cold water.

2 When cold, peel off the skin. Cut the tomatoes crosswise in half and squeeze out the seeds, then finely chop the tomatoes.

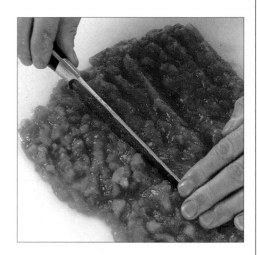

Use sharp chef's knife to cut cleanly through fennel bulb

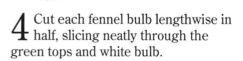

3 Trim the fennel stalks and root, discarding any tough outer pieces from the bulb. Reserve some green fronds for decoration.

4 Cut each fennel bulb lengthwise in half, slicing neatly through the green tops and white bulb.

5 Set each fennel half flat-side down on the chopping board and cut it into thin slices using the chef's knife.

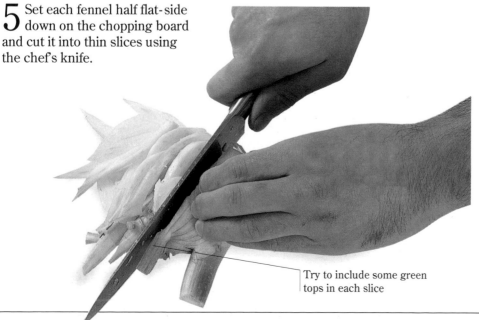

Try to include some green tops in each slice

6 Set the flat side of the chef's knife on top of each garlic clove and strike it with your fist. Discard the skin and finely chop the garlic.

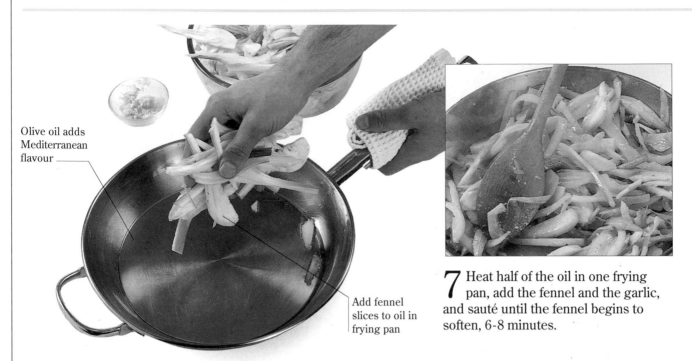

Olive oil adds Mediterranean flavour

Add fennel slices to oil in frying pan

7 Heat half of the oil in one frying pan, add the fennel and the garlic, and sauté until the fennel begins to soften, 6-8 minutes.

8 Add three-quarters of the tomatoes, the pastis, salt, and pepper to the pan and cook, stirring occasionally, until the mixture is thick and most of the moisture has evaporated, 20-25 minutes. Taste for seasoning.

9 Meanwhile, trim the excess fat from each of the lamb chops. Cut off the "tail" of each. Season both sides of each chop with salt and pepper.

Turn chops with palette knife

10 Heat the remaining oil in the second frying pan, add the chops and tails, and cook over high heat until well browned, 1-2 minutes. Turn and brown the other side.

ANNE SAYS
"The chops should only be browned on the outside at this point; cooking will continue in the oven."

11 Transfer the chops and tails to the plate and set aside.

2 MAKE THE PAPER CASES

1 Fold a large sheet of parchment paper measuring about 30 x 37.5 cm (12 x 15 inches) in half and draw a curve to make a heart shape when unfolded, and large enough to leave a 7.5 cm (3 inch) border around a chop.

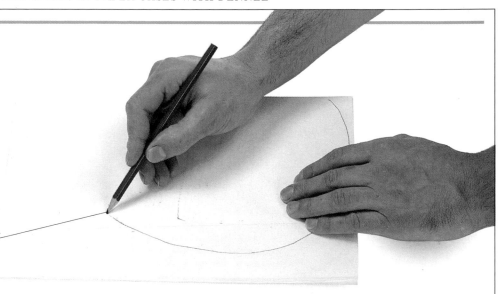

Draw shape lightly with pencil

2 Cut out the heart shape with scissors. Repeat to make a total of 4 paper hearts.

ANNE SAYS

"Aluminium foil is a practical alternative to parchment paper for the parcels, but the presentation is less impressive because the foil does not puff and brown like paper."

3 Open out the paper hearts and brush each one with melted butter, leaving a border of about 2.5 cm (1 inch) unbuttered.

4 For the glaze, use the fork to beat the egg with the salt until mixed. Brush the egg glaze on the unbuttered border of each paper heart.

Egg glaze will give airtight seal to parcels

3 FILL THE PAPER CASES AND BAKE

Fronds from fennel bulbs give aniseed flavour

1 Heat the oven to 190°C (375°F, Gas 5). Spoon a bed of the fennel mixture on one half of a paper heart.

2 Set a lamb chop and tail on top of the fennel mixture.

3 Spoon a little of the reserved chopped tomato over the lamb chop and lay a fennel frond on top.

Second half of paper heart will enclose chop and vegetables

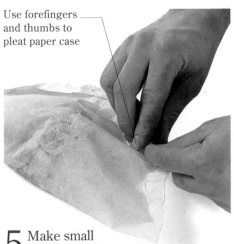

Use forefingers and thumbs to pleat paper case

4 Fold the paper over the filling and run your fingers along the edge of the paper to stick the 2 sides of the heart together.

5 Make small pleats to seal the edges of the paper case.

6 Twist the ends of the paper case to finish. Repeat the process with the remaining ingredients to make 4 paper parcels.

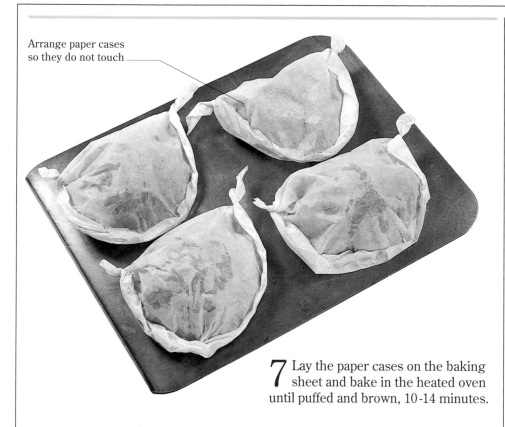

Arrange paper cases
so they do not touch

7 Lay the paper cases on the baking
sheet and bake in the heated oven
until puffed and brown, 10-14 minutes.

¶⦿¶ TO SERVE
Transfer the puffed, browned paper
parcels to warmed individual plates,
leaving each person to open his or her
own parcel. Serve at once while the
parcels are still puffed.

ANNE SAYS
*"If the paper parcels cool and deflate
after being taken from the oven, they can
be puffed again by briefly warming them
in the oven."*

Fennel partners
lamb well

**Lamb chop and
vegetables** in
paper case make
complete meal

V A R I A T I O N
LAMB CHOPS IN PAPER CASES WITH LEEKS

*Here the lamb chops are baked
on a bed of leeks, tomatoes, and
herbs cooked in white wine.*

1 Prepare the tomatoes and garlic as
directed; omit the fennel.
2 Trim 500 g (1 lb) leeks, discarding
the root and the tough green tops. Slit
them lengthwise, wash them
thoroughly under running water in a
colander, drain well, and slice them.
3 Strip the leaves from 3-5 sprigs of
fresh rosemary or thyme, setting aside
4 small sprigs. Pile the leaves on a
chopping board and finely chop them
with a chef's knife.
4 Heat the oil in a frying pan and add
the garlic, leeks, and all the tomatoes
with 125 ml (4 fl oz) dry white wine,
salt, and pepper. Continue as directed,
omitting the pastis. Stir in the chopped
herbs at the end of cooking.
5 Brown the lamb chops, make the
paper cases, and fill as directed,
topping each chop with a reserved
herb sprig. Bake and serve
immediately.

FILLET OF BEEF STUFFED WITH MUSHROOMS

🍽 SERVES 8-10   🥣 WORK TIME 50-55 MINUTES*   ♨ COOKING TIME ABOUT 1-1¼ HOURS

EQUIPMENT

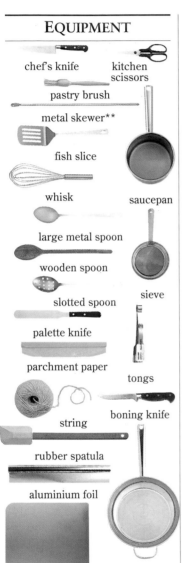

chef's knife
kitchen scissors
pastry brush
metal skewer**
fish slice
whisk
saucepan
large metal spoon
wooden spoon
slotted spoon
sieve
palette knife
parchment paper
tongs
string
boning knife
rubber spatula
aluminium foil
baking sheet
frying pans
roasting tin
food processor   lemon squeezer

** meat thermometer can be used

Fillet of beef is a cut for a special occasion – lean, tender, and easy to carve. Here it is partially sliced and stuffed with a "duxelles" of mushrooms, parsley, garlic, and bacon.

GETTING AHEAD
The beef can be roasted and stuffed up to 12 hours ahead and stored in the refrigerator, with the Madeira sauce. Reheat the beef and sauce just before serving.

plus about 2 hours cooling time

metric	SHOPPING LIST	imperial
1	fillet of beef, weighing about 2.3 kg (5 lb) untrimmed or 1.6 kg (3½ lb) trimmed	1
	salt and pepper	
30 ml	vegetable oil	2 tbsp
750 ml	beef or brown veal stock (see box, page 36)	1¼ pints
1	bunch of watercress	1
8-10	large button mushrooms	8-10
30 g	butter, more for parchment paper	1 oz
	juice of ½ lemon	
250 ml	water, more if needed	8 fl oz
15 ml	arrowroot	1 tbsp
125 ml	Madeira	4 fl oz
For the stuffing		
2	shallots	2
125 g	streaky bacon	4 oz
3	garlic cloves	3
500 g	mushrooms	1 lb
1	medium bunch of parsley	1

INGREDIENTS

fillet of beef
streaky bacon   mushrooms
watercress
parsley
beef stock   shallots
butter
vegetable oil   Madeira
arrowroot   lemon juice   garlic cloves

ORDER OF WORK

1 TRIM AND ROAST THE BEEF

2 PREPARE THE STUFFING

3 STUFF AND REHEAT THE BEEF

4 MAKE THE GARNISH AND FINISH THE DISH

1 TRIM AND ROAST THE BEEF

Tough membrane
must be removed
from fillet before
cooking

1 Heat the oven
to 230°C (450°F,
Gas 8). To trim the beef,
cut and pull away the fat
to expose the meat. Cut
away the chain muscle
that lies to the side of
the main part of the fillet.
Using the boning knife,
slit the tight skin of
membrane enclosing
the fillet and cut it away,
leaving the red tender
meat lying beneath it.

ANNE SAYS
*"The chain muscle is tough but can be
used, after trimming, for stews or
minced beef recipes."*

2 If the tail, or tapered end, of the
fillet is included, fold it under
to make an even cylinder of
the meat.

ANNE SAYS
*"A piece of meat of uniform
thickness will cook evenly."*

3 Tie one piece of string lengthwise
around the fillet. Using separate
pieces of string, tie the roll at 2.5 cm
(1 inch) intervals.

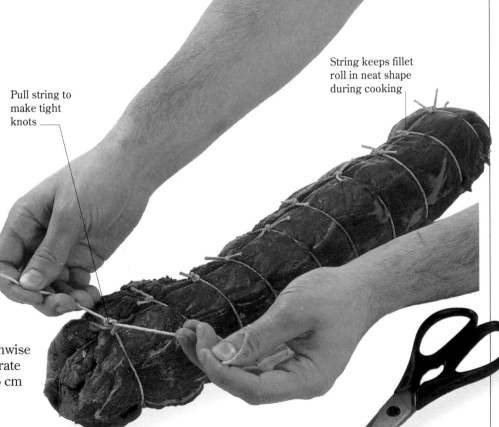

Pull string to
make tight
knots

String keeps fillet
roll in neat shape
during cooking

Turn with tongs so meat is not pierced

Sear meat to make crisp crust on outside

4 Sprinkle the beef with salt and pepper. To sear the meat, heat the oil in the large roasting tin on top of the stove until very hot, then brown the fillet well on all sides, turning it with the tongs. Transfer the beef to the heated oven.

5 Roast the fillet of beef, allowing 12-15 minutes for rare meat or 18-20 minutes for medium-done. For rare, the skewer inserted in the centre of the meat will be cool to the touch when withdrawn after 30 seconds; for medium-done, it will be warm. Or, test with a meat thermometer: it will register 52°C (125°F) for rare meat and 60°C (140°F) for medium-done.

ANNE SAYS
"Cooking time depends on the shape – a long thin fillet will cook more quickly than a short, plump one."

6 Remove the beef, let it cool, and then chill it until cold, at least 2 hours. Discard any fat from the roasting tin. Add half of the beef stock and boil, stirring to dissolve the juices in the tin. Strain the juices back into the remaining stock and set aside.

2 PREPARE THE STUFFING

1 Peel the shallots and cut them into quarters. Stack the bacon rashers and cut across into 2.5 cm (1 inch) pieces. Set the flat side of the chef's knife on top of each garlic clove and strike it with your fist. Discard the skin.

2 Put the shallots, garlic, and bacon in the food processor and finely chop them to a paste. Alternatively, finely chop them with the chef's knife. Transfer to a frying pan.

Food processor makes chopping very quick

Parsley leaves
enhance flavour
of stuffing

3 Wipe the mushroom caps with a damp paper towel and trim the stalks. Cut the caps into quarters. Chop them in the food processor, using the pulse button. Alternatively, chop them with the chef's knife.

4 Strip the parsley leaves from the stalks and pile them on the chopping board. With the chef's knife cut them into pieces, then, holding the tip of the blade against the board, rock it back and forth to finely chop them.

Keep parsley
stalks for adding
to bouquet garni

5 Heat the shallot, garlic, and bacon mixture in the frying pan, stirring with the wooden spoon, until the mixture begins to brown, 2-3 minutes.

6 Add the chopped mushrooms, salt, and pepper and cook over high heat, stirring occasionally, until all the moisture has evaporated, 10-15 minutes.

7 Stir the chopped parsley into the mixture. Taste the stuffing for seasoning. Let it cool, then chill.

3 STUFF AND REHEAT THE BEEF

1 Heat the oven to 220°C (425°F, Gas 7). When the fillet is cold, remove and discard the strings. Slice the beef at 1 cm (1/2 inch) intervals, cutting not quite through the fillet so that the underside remains attached.

2 Set the fillet on top of a sheet of heavy-duty foil. With the palette knife, spread 15-30 ml (1-2 tbsp) of the stuffing between each slice and press the fillet back into its original shape.

Open cuts in fillet so stuffing can be inserted

3 Wrap the fillet in the foil, making a neat cylinder and twisting the ends of the foil to make handles. Set the fillet on the baking sheet and put in the heated oven. For rare beef, allow 15-20 minutes; the skewer inserted in the centre of the meat will be cool to the touch when withdrawn after 30 seconds and a meat thermometer will register 52°C (125°F). For medium-done, allow 20-25 minutes; the skewer will be warm when withdrawn and a thermometer will register 60°C (140°F). Meanwhile, make the garnish.

4 MAKE THE GARNISH AND FINISH THE DISH

1 Rinse the watercress in cold water, drain, and dry thoroughly with paper towels. Discard the stalk ends.

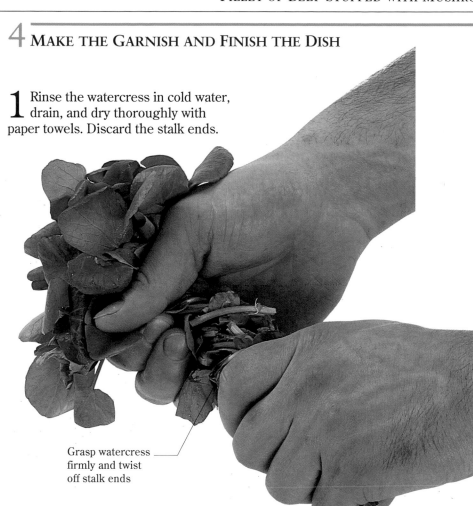

Grasp watercress firmly and twist off stalk ends

2 Wipe the mushroom caps with a damp paper towel; trim the stalks even with the caps. With the point of a small knife, make 5 or 6 impressions in the top of each mushroom to create a star design.

ANNE SAYS
"It is easy to make a well-defined indentation in the tender mushroom cap using the tip of a knife, and this is a simple way of creating an attractive garnish with a professional finish."

3 Put the mushroom caps, star-side down, in a frying pan with the butter, lemon juice, salt, pepper, and enough water to cover them partially.

4 Make a paper round: fold a square of parchment paper in half and then in half again to make a triangle. Fold the triangle over once or twice or more to form a slender cone. Holding the tip of the cone over the centre of the pan, cut the cone, using the edge of the pan as a guide. Unfold the round.

Hold paper cone over pan with tip at centre

5 Butter the paper round and place it over the mushrooms in the frying pan, buttered-side down. Simmer them until tender, 15-20 minutes, then remove them with the slotted spoon and keep warm.

6 Put the stock in the saucepan and pour in the mushroom cooking liquid. Bring to a boil and cook until reduced by half.

7 Put the arrowroot in a small bowl and stir in 30 ml (2 tbsp) of the Madeira to form a smooth paste.

Lightly rest edge of baking sheet on rim of pan

8 Whisk the arrowroot paste into the boiling stock. It will thicken at once. Stir in the remaining Madeira and taste the sauce for seasoning.

9 Cut a slit in one end of the foil parcel and drain any juices into the sauce. Whisk the sauce to mix in the juices, then keep it warm over very low heat.

10 Cut open the foil and transfer the fillet to a carving board.

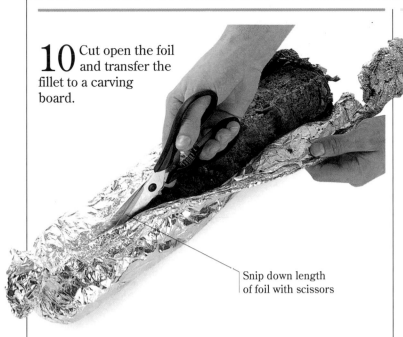

Snip down length of foil with scissors

🍽️ **TO SERVE**
Cut the fillet into slices and arrange on a warmed platter. Garnish with the sautéed mushroom caps and watercress, as well as asparagus if you like, and pass the sauce separately.

Tender beef has rich mushroom filling

Fresh asparagus beautifully complements this elegant dinner party dish

VARIATION

TOURNEDOS OF BEEF WITH MUSHROOMS

Here the beef is cut into steaks – called tournedos – which are seared, then spread with the mushroom stuffing. Instead of the more traditional fried bread, these are served on turnip rounds and topped with the Madeira sauce.

1 Prepare the mushroom stuffing and mushroom garnish as directed in the main recipe.
2 Peel 2-3 large turnips and cut them into 8 rounds, each 1 cm (1/2 inch) thick. (The rounds should be the same diameter as the tournedos.) Put the rounds in a pan of cold salted water, bring to a boil, and simmer until just tender, 5-7 minutes. Drain thoroughly and set aside.
3 Trim the fillet of beef and tie it in a cylinder with individual pieces of string. Cut between the strings to form 8 steaks of even thickness.
4 Heat 15 ml (1 tbsp) oil in a large frying pan until very hot. Sprinkle the steaks on both sides with salt and pepper, add them to the pan, and fry until well browned, 3-4 minutes. Turn the steaks with the tongs and continue frying until the steaks are done to your taste. To test, press the top of the steak with your finger; for rare (3-4 minutes on the second side), the meat will yield like a damp sponge; for medium (5-6 minutes on the second side), the meat will resist slightly. If the meat is firm, it is well done and will be tough.
5 Transfer the steaks to a plate and pour off any fat from the pan. Add the stock and boil, stirring to dissolve the pan juices, until reduced by half. Make the arrowroot paste as directed and whisk in with the remaining Madeira; taste for seasoning.
6 Put the turnip rounds on individual warmed plates; top with the tournedos. Reheat the stuffing if necessary; spread it on the meat. Set a mushroom on top, pour sauce around the meat, and garnish with watercress. Serve immediately.

ROAST LEG OF LAMB WITH HARICOT BEANS

Gigot d'Agneau à la Bretonne

🍽 SERVES 6-8 🥄 WORK TIME 35-40 MINUTES* ♨ COOKING TIME 1½-2 HOURS

EQUIPMENT

small knife

large flameproof casserole

chef's knife

boning knife

colander

large metal spoon

fish slice

wooden spoon

slotted spoon

bowls

chopping board   2-pronged fork

carving knife

roasting tin

aluminium foil

metal skewer**

** meat thermometer can also be used

A good roast leg of lamb is unbeatable for flavour and succulence. This version is served Brittany style, studded with garlic and accompanied by the haricot beans for which Brittany is famous.

* plus 8-12 hours soaking time for beans

INGREDIENTS

leg of lamb

carrots

beef stock   fresh rosemary

 garlic cloves

vegetable oil

bouquet garni

white wine

onions

whole cloves

dried haricot beans

ANNE SAYS
"*When choosing a leg of lamb, ask your butcher for a small leg, which has had the pelvic bone removed to make carving easy.*"

ORDER OF WORK

1 SOAK AND COOK THE BEANS

2 PREPARE AND ROAST THE LAMB

3 FINISH THE DISH

metric	SHOPPING LIST	imperial
1	leg of lamb, weighing about 2.7 kg (6 lb)	1
2	garlic cloves	2
1	onion	1
1	carrot	1
2-3	sprigs of fresh rosemary	2-3
45 ml	vegetable oil	3 tbsp
125 ml	white wine	4 fl oz
250 ml	beef or brown veal stock (see box, page 36) or water, more if needed	8 fl oz
	salt and pepper	
	For the beans	
500 g	dried haricot beans	1 lb
1	onion	1
2	whole cloves	2
1	carrot	1
1	bouquet garni made with 5-6 parsley stalks, 2-3 sprigs of fresh thyme, and 1 bay leaf	1
2-3	sprigs of parsley (optional)	2-3
	baked tomatoes (see box, page 63) for serving (optional)	

1 SOAK AND COOK THE BEANS

Herbs, clove-studded onion, and carrots add flavour to beans

1 Put the dried haricot beans in a bowl, pour in cold water to cover, and let soak overnight.

ANNE SAYS

"If you are short of time, instead of soaking the beans, put them in a pan, add water to cover, and simmer 1 hour."

2 Peel the onion and stud with the cloves. Peel, trim, then cut the carrot into quarters.

3 Drain the beans and put them in the casserole; add the clove-studded onion, carrot, bouquet garni, and enough water to cover by at least 2.5 cm (1 inch).

Test bean for tenderness between fingers

4 Bring to a boil, cover, and simmer, skimming as necessary, 1½-2 hours. Add hot water, as needed, to keep the beans covered. Season with salt and pepper halfway through cooking. When cooked, the beans should be tender, but not mushy. While the beans are cooking, roast the lamb.

5 When the beans are tender, remove the onion, carrot, and bouquet garni from the casserole and discard them.

HOW TO CHOP HERBS

Parsley, dill, chives, rosemary, tarragon, and basil are herbs that are usually chopped before being added to other ingredients. Do not chop delicate herbs like basil too finely because they bruise easily.

1 Strip the leaves or sprigs from the stalks. Pile the leaves or sprigs on a chopping board.

2 Cut the leaves or sprigs into small pieces. Holding the tip of the blade against the board and rocking the knife back and forth, continue chopping until the herbs are coarse or fine, as you wish.

ANNE SAYS
"Make sure that your knife is very sharp, otherwise you will bruise the herbs rather than cut them."

2 PREPARE AND ROAST THE LAMB

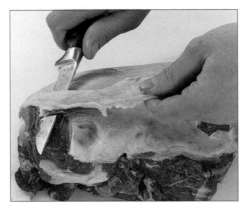

1 Heat the oven to 230°C (450°F, Gas 8). Using the boning knife, trim the skin and fat from the lamb.

2 Peel the garlic and cut each clove into 4-5 thin slivers. Make several shallow incisions in the lamb with the point of the small knife. Insert the slivers of garlic in the little pockets.

3 Peel and quarter the onion and carrot and put them in the roasting tin. Set the lamb on top. Coarsely chop the rosemary (see box, left). Pour the oil over the lamb and sprinkle with the rosemary, salt, and pepper.

4 Sear the lamb in the heated oven until browned, 10-15 minutes.

ANNE SAYS
"Searing forms a crust around the meat and seals in the juices."

Flavour of rosemary permeates meat

5 Lower the oven to 180°C (350°F, Gas 4) and continue roasting, basting often, 1-1¼ hours for rare meat or 1¼-1½ hours for medium done. When rare, the skewer inserted in the meat 30 seconds will be cool to the touch when withdrawn. A meat thermometer will show 52°C (125°F). When the meat is medium done, the skewer will be warm and a meat thermometer will show 60°C (140°F).

Basting ensures that meat browns and stays moist

ANNE SAYS
"If the cooking juices start to brown too much, add a little water."

BAKED TOMATOES

In Brittany, baked tomatoes are the traditional accompaniment to roast lamb, baked while the roast stands.

🍴 SERVES 6-8

🥣 WORK TIME 10 MINUTES

♨ COOKING TIME 12-15 MINUTES

SHOPPING LIST

45 ml	olive oil, more for dish	3 tbsp
4	large tomatoes, total weight about 1 kg (2 lb)	4
2	garlic cloves	2
2-3	sprigs of parsley	2-3
60 g	dried breadcrumbs	2 oz
	salt and pepper	

1 Heat the oven to 190°C (375°F, Gas 5). Oil a baking dish. Cut the cores from the tomatoes and cut them in half horizontally. If necessary, cut a small slice off the base of each tomato half so it sits flat.

2 Set the flat side of a chef's knife on top of each garlic clove and strike it with your fist. Discard the skin and finely chop the garlic. Finely chop the parsley. Mix together the garlic, breadcrumbs, parsley, and oil. Season well with salt and pepper.

3 Set the tomato halves in the prepared baking dish and spoon the crumb-herb mixture on each half. Bake in the heated oven until the tops are browned and the tomatoes are tender, 12-15 minutes.

Topping is crisp and golden brown

Cooked tomatoes have tender flesh

3 FINISH THE DISH

1 When the lamb is cooked to your taste, transfer it to a serving platter.

Use fish slice and 2-pronged fork to transfer meat

2 Cover the lamb with foil and let stand 10-15 minutes (this will make the meat easier to carve).

3 Make the gravy. Discard the excess fat from the roasting tin, leaving the carrot and onion.

4 Add the wine to the tin and boil the cooking juices and wine until reduced by half.

5 Add the stock and boil, stirring to dissolve the juices in the tin, until the gravy is concentrated and well flavoured, 5-10 minutes. Strain the gravy into a gravy boat and keep it in a warm place.

Stock dissolves caramelized cooking juices to form savoury gravy

6 Reheat the beans if necessary. Finely chop the parsley and sprinkle it on the beans, if you like.

VARIATION

LEMON ROAST LEG OF LAMB WITH COURGETTE GRATINS

Lemon zest is inserted with the garlic slivers for this roast leg of lamb, which is served with individual baked courgette and Gruyère custards.

7 Carve the lamb into thin slices using the carving knife and 2-pronged fork.

TO SERVE
Arrange the lamb on warmed plates. Spoon the beans next to the lamb slices and accompany with baked tomatoes, if you like. Serve the gravy separately.

1 Omit the beans and rosemary.
2 Trim the lamb as directed in the main recipe and peel and sliver the garlic. Peel the zest from 1 large lemon with a vegetable peeler and cut half of the zest into pieces the size of the garlic slivers. Cut the remaining zest into fine julienne; blanch in boiling water 1 minute, then drain and reserve for the garnish. Insert 2 pieces of lemon zest with each garlic sliver in the incisions in the meat. Squeeze the juice from the lemon and reserve for the gravy.
3 Roast the leg of lamb as directed.
4 Meanwhile, trim 4 courgettes (total weight about 750 g/1½ lb) and cut them into 1 cm (½ inch) slices. Blanch in a pan of boiling salted water 1 minute. Drain, rinse with cold water, and drain again thoroughly. Pat dry on paper towels and arrange them in 6 oiled gratin dishes.
5 Grate 30 g (1 oz) Gruyère cheese. Whisk together 2 eggs, 250 ml (8 fl oz) double cream, three-quarters of the grated cheese, salt, and pepper. Pour the mixture over the courgettes and sprinkle with the remaining cheese.
6 When the lamb is removed from the oven, cover with foil and let stand in a warm place until the gratins are cooked. Bake the courgette gratins until the egg mixture is just set and the tops are golden brown, 10-15 minutes.
7 Make the gravy as directed, stirring in the lemon juice just before serving.
8 Sprinkle the reserved lemon zest julienne over the lamb when serving and accompany each serving with a courgette gratin.

Roast leg of lamb is carved into lean, juicy slices

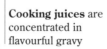

Cooking juices are concentrated in flavourful gravy

Haricot beans are classic French accompaniment

GETTING AHEAD
The beans can be cooked up to 2 days ahead and kept, covered, in the refrigerator; reheat them on top of the stove. It is best not to roast the lamb in advance, however.

ITALIAN BRAISED VEAL

Osso Buco

 🍴 SERVES 4-6 WORK TIME 30-35 MINUTES 🍲 COOKING TIME 1½-2 HOURS

EQUIPMENT

2-pronged fork

vegetable peeler

large sauté pan with lid*

chef's knife

grater

small plate

sieve

wooden spoon

bowls

slotted spoon

large plate

chopping board

* deep frying pan or flameproof casserole with lid can also be used

INGREDIENTS

veal shin

canned Italian plum tomatoes**

carrot

onions

orange

lemon

garlic clove

butter

vegetable oil

parsley

white veal stock

white wine

plain flour

** fresh plum tomatoes can also be used

In this classic dish from Milan, thick pieces of veal shin are braised with vegetables, white wine, and stock, which form a rich sauce. A zesty mixture called "gremolata" is sprinkled on top just before serving. An excellent accompaniment is risotto Milanese, made with rice, Parmesan cheese, and saffron.

metric	SHOPPING LIST	imperial
400 g	can of Italian plum tomatoes	14 oz
1	garlic clove	1
1	orange	1
2	onions	2
1	carrot	1
30 g	plain flour	1 oz
	salt and pepper	
4-6	pieces of veal shin with bones, about 1.8 kg (4 lb)	4-6
30 ml	vegetable oil	2 tbsp
30 g	butter	1 oz
250 ml	white wine	8 fl oz
125 ml	white veal stock (see box, page 36) or water, more if needed	4 fl oz
	For the gremolata	
1	small bunch of parsley	1
1	lemon	1
1	garlic clove	1

ORDER OF WORK

1 PREPARE THE INGREDIENTS

2 BRAISE THE VEAL

3 MAKE THE GREMOLATA

1 PREPARE THE INGREDIENTS

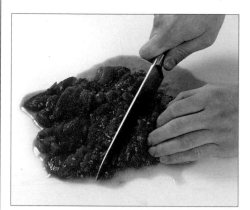

1 Heat the oven to 180°C (350°F, Gas 4). Tip the canned tomatoes into the sieve set over a bowl and drain off as much liquid as possible. Transfer the drained tomatoes to the chopping board and coarsely chop them with the chef's knife.

ANNE SAYS

"*If using fresh tomatoes, cut out the cores and score an "x" on the base of each. Immerse in boiling water until the skin starts to split. Transfer at once to cold water. When cold, peel off the skin, cut crosswise in half, and squeeze out the seeds. Chop coarsely.*"

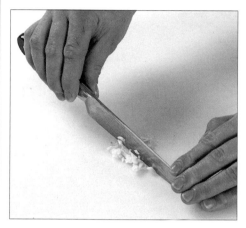

2 Set the flat side of the chef's knife on top of the garlic clove and strike it with your fist. Discard the skin and finely chop the garlic.

3 Grate the zest from the orange. Finely chop the onions (see box, page 68).

Guide knife with fingers of your other hand

4 Peel and trim the carrot. Cut it lengthwise into quarters and then across into thin slices.

Flour coating will seal in juices during cooking

5 Put the flour on a large plate, season it with salt and pepper, and stir to combine. Lightly coat the veal pieces with the seasoned flour, patting to ensure flour adheres.

HOW TO CHOP AN ONION

The size of dice when chopping an onion depends on the thickness of the initial slices. For a standard size, make slices about 5 mm (1/4 inch) thick. For finely chopped onions, slice as thinly as possible.

1 Peel the onion and trim the top; leave a little of the root attached. Cut the onion lengthwise in half, through root and stalk.

2 Put one onion half, cut-side down, on a chopping board. Using a chef's knife, make a series of horizontal cuts from the top towards the root, but not through it.

3 Make a series of lengthwise vertical cuts, cutting just to the root but not through it. Slice the onion crosswise to obtain dice.

2 BRAISE THE VEAL

Veal browns evenly if pan is not crowded

1 Heat the oil and butter in the sauté pan, add the veal pieces, in batches if necessary, and brown thoroughly on all sides. Transfer to a plate with the slotted spoon.

ANNE SAYS
"The pan should not be crowded or the meat will steam rather than brown, so if necessary, brown it in batches."

2 Discard all but 30 ml (2 tbsp) fat from the pan. Add the chopped carrot and onions, and cook, stirring occasionally, until soft. Add the wine and boil until it has reduced by half.

3 Stir in the tomatoes, garlic, grated orange zest, salt, and pepper. Lay the veal on top.

Stock keeps veal moist

4 Pour in the veal stock, then cover the pan and cook in the heated oven until the veal is very tender when pierced with the 2-pronged fork, 1 1/2-2 hours. Add more stock during cooking if the pan gets dry. At the end of cooking the sauce should be thick and rich. If necessary, boil to reduce and thicken it.

3 MAKE THE GREMOLATA

1 Strip the parsley leaves from the stalks and pile them on the chopping board. With the chef's knife, finely chop the leaves, holding the tip of the knife against the board and rocking the blade back and forth. Put them in a small bowl.

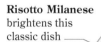

2 Grate the zest from the lemon into the bowl containing the parsley. Chop the garlic and add to the bowl. Stir the ingredients together.

Grate only coloured zest from lemon peel

🍽️ TO SERVE

Transfer the veal slices to individual plates, spoon the sauce on top, and sprinkle with the gremolata.

Risotto Milanese brightens this classic dish

Gremolata of parsley, lemon, and garlic enhances taste and colour

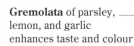

V A R I A T I O N

FRENCH BRAISED LAMB

In this recipe, called Jarret d'Agneau in France, knuckles of lamb are cooked in a red wine sauce.

1 Prepare the garlic, orange zest, onions, and carrot as directed in the main recipe; omit the tomatoes. Trim the excess fat from 6-8 knuckles of lamb, weighing about 375 g (12 oz) each.
2 Brown the lamb on all sides, then braise as directed, substituting red for white wine, and cooking until tender, 2-2½ hours.
3 Omit the gremolata. Peel, deseed, and finely chop 4 fresh plum tomatoes, or chop 250 g (8 oz) drained canned Italian plum tomatoes. Chop 2 garlic cloves and the leaves from 3-5 sprigs of fresh rosemary.
4 If you like, scrape the ends of the lamb bones clean, and arrange like the spokes of a wheel on a serving platter. Mix together the tomatoes, garlic, and rosemary and sprinkle over the lamb just before serving.

GETTING AHEAD

The veal can be cooked up to 3 days ahead and kept, covered, in the refrigerator, or can be frozen. Reheat on top of the stove until bubbling; sprinkle with gremolata before serving.

AUNT SALLY'S MEAT LOAF

EQUIPMENT

boning knife

fork   chef's knife

wooden spoon

palette knife

metal skewer

23 x 13 x 7.5 cm
(9 x 5 x 3 inch)
loaf tin

bowl

large plate

small frying pan

medium saucepan

plate

food processor

colander

large
mixing
bowl

mincer

Meat loaf is a true American classic with numerous variations. Here the addition of spinach, bacon, plenty of seasonings, and a big shake of Worcestershire sauce gives a fresh accent. Mashed potato is the ideal accompaniment to Aunt Sally's Meat Loaf, with ketchup or homemade cranberry sauce for a piquant aside.

GETTING AHEAD

The meat loaf can be made 2 days ahead and kept, covered, in the refrigerator. Reheat 20-25 minutes in an oven heated to 180°C (350°F, Gas 4), or slice cold for sandwiches.

metric	SHOPPING LIST	imperial
175 g	fresh spinach	6 oz
750 g	braising steak	1½ lb
250 g	boned veal shoulder	8 oz
375 g	streaky bacon rashers (without rind)	12 oz
1	large onion	1
3-4	sprigs of fresh thyme	3-4
3-4	sprigs of fresh rosemary	3-4
4	garlic cloves	4
2	eggs	2
6	slices of white bread	6
15 ml	Worcestershire sauce	1 tbsp
	salt and pepper	

INGREDIENTS

boned veal
shoulder*

spinach

braising steak**

fresh rosemary

fresh thyme

streaky
bacon

garlic cloves

Worcestershire
sauce

white bread

eggs

onion

* minced veal can also be used

** minced beef can also be used

ORDER OF WORK

1 PREPARE THE
INGREDIENTS

2 MIX AND BAKE THE
MEAT LOAF

1 PREPARE THE INGREDIENTS

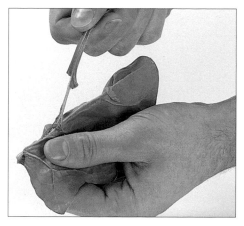

Squeezing removes maximum water

1 Remove tough ribs and stalks from the spinach. Wash it well. Half-fill the saucepan with water and bring to a boil. Add salt, then add the spinach and simmer until tender, 2-3 minutes.

2 Drain the spinach in the colander, rinse with cold water, and drain again thoroughly. Squeeze the spinach in your hand to remove all excess water, then chop.

4 Work the beef, veal, and bacon pieces through fine blade of the mincer.

ANNE SAYS
"You can also use the food processor to mince the meat: cut the meat into smaller cubes and mince it with short pulses. Do not overwork the meat or it will be tough when cooked."

Feed cubes of meat into machine in small batches

3 If using braising steak and veal shoulder, trim off any fat and sinew. Cut the beef and veal into large chunks. Cut the bacon into large pieces, reserving 4 rashers for topping the loaf.

HOW TO PEEL AND CHOP GARLIC CLOVES

1 To separate the bulb, crush with the heel of your hand. Or, pull out a clove with your fingers. To peel the clove, lightly crush with the flat of a chef's knife to loosen the skin.

2 Peel off the skin with your fingers. Set the flat side of the knife on top of the clove and strike firmly with your fist.

3 Finely chop the garlic clove with the chef's knife, moving the blade back and forth.

5 Peel the onion, leaving a little of the root attached, and cut it in half. Slice each half horizontally, leaving the slices attached at the root end, then slice vertically, again leaving the root end uncut. Cut across to make dice.

6 Strip the thyme and rosemary leaves from the stalks and pile them on the chopping board. With the chef's knife, finely chop the leaves. Peel and finely chop the garlic cloves (see box, page 71).

7 Lightly beat the eggs in a small bowl. Trim and discard the crusts from the bread. Work the bread slices in the food processor or a blender to form crumbs, then tip into a large bowl.

2 MIX AND BAKE THE MEAT LOAF

1 Heat the oven to 180°C (350°F, Gas 4). Add the minced meat, chopped spinach, onion, garlic, thyme, rosemary, Worcestershire sauce, salt, and pepper to the large bowl and combine with the wooden spoon.

Mixture is lightly bound with beaten egg

Pack mixture tightly into loaf tin for even baking

2 Add the beaten eggs to the mixture in the bowl and lightly mix them in.

3 To test for seasoning, fry a spoonful of the mixture in the frying pan until browned on both sides. Taste it and add more seasoning to the remaining meat mixture if necessary. Transfer the mixture to the loaf tin, pressing it down and patting it with the wooden spoon to smooth the top.

1 ROAST THE PORK

1 Heat the oven to 180°C (350°F, Gas 4). Wipe the pork with paper towels, then set it in the roasting tin.

2 Cut 6 of the oranges in half and squeeze out the juice. There should be about 500 ml (16 fl oz).

ANNE SAYS
"You can also buy freshly squeezed orange juice."

3 Pour some of the orange juice over the pork and roast in the heated oven 3-3¹/₂ hours, pouring more orange juice over the joint about every 30 minutes to keep it moist.

4 Meanwhile, cut the remaining oranges in half vertically and cut off the ends. Cut each half into neat slices, discarding any pips.

Pour orange juice over whole of joint

Basting with orange juice adds flavour and keeps pork moist

5 To test if the pork is cooked, insert the skewer for 30 seconds; it should be warm to the touch when withdrawn. A meat thermometer should show 77°C (170°F).

! TAKE CARE !
Test in the centre of the meat near, but not touching, the bone.

2 GLAZE THE PORK; MAKE THE SAUCE

Spoon on sugar and mustard mixture and press onto fat with palette knife

1 Take the pork from the oven and let it cool slightly. Increase the heat to 200°C (400°F, Gas 6). Cut through the skin around the bone end of the joint. With the help of the knife, peel the skin from the fat, starting from the wider end of the joint.

2 Mix the mustard and brown sugar together in a bowl. Spread and press the mixture over the pork, so that it clings to the fat.

3 Overlap the halved orange slices over the joint. Stud each piece of orange with a clove, taking care that the cloves do not break.

4 Continue roasting the pork until the surface has a shiny glaze, 30-45 minutes. Baste the pork with the juices in the tin every 10 minutes, adding more orange juice if needed.

5 Transfer the pork to a warmed large serving platter. Remove the orange slices and arrange them on the platter next to the pork. Cover with foil and keep warm.

6 Pour the Grand Marnier into the juices in the roasting tin. Bring to a boil and whisk to dissolve the juices. If the sauce is too thick, add more orange juice.

7 Add the nutmeg and ground cloves to the sauce and mix them in with the whisk. Transfer to a sauce boat.

3 CARVE THE PORK

1 Insert the 2-pronged fork in the pork, at the shin or bone end of the joint. With the chef's knife, make a vertical slice near the shin end, cutting down to the bone, holding the joint steady with the fork. Make 3-4 more vertical slices down to the bone, each about 1 cm (1/2 inch) apart.

2 Re-insert the knife at the first slice and curve the knife to slide along the bone, detaching the slices. Continue slicing remaining pork in the same way.

Hold joint steady with 2-pronged fork while slicing

🍴 TO SERVE
Arrange the slices of pork on individual warmed plates with the halved orange slices and add a bouquet of watercress to each. Spoon some sauce over each serving of meat and serve the rest separately.

Glazed pork has delicious fresh sweet accent

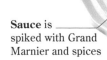

Sauce is spiked with Grand Marnier and spices

ROAST LEG OF PORK WITH APPLES

Here pork is basted with apple juice during roasting, and small apples stuffed with brown sugar and sultanas are baked to accompany the pork.

1 Roast the pork as directed, basting with 750 ml (1 1/4 pints) apple juice in place of the orange juice.

2 Omit the orange slices. Instead, scrub 8-10 small Golden Delicious apples (total weight about 1.8 kg/4 lb) under cold water and core each with an apple corer or vegetable peeler. Cut a slice from the end of the core and replace it in the bottom of the apple so the filling does not leak out during baking. With a knife, score each apple in a horizontal circle so it does not burst during baking.

3 Remove the pork skin, spread with the mustard and brown sugar mixture, and stud the cloves into the pork.

4 Mix 90 g (3 oz) sultanas with 100 g (3 1/2 oz) dark soft brown sugar. Stuff each apple and arrange in the roasting tin around the pork. Continue roasting as directed, basting both the pork and apples every 10 minutes.

5 Transfer the roast pork to the serving platter. Make the sauce as directed, adding brandy in place of the Grand Marnier and more apple juice if needed. Add an extra 30-45 ml (2-3 tbsp) sultanas and simmer in the sauce about 2 minutes.

6 Carve the pork as directed and serve with the baked apples and sauce.

INDIAN BRAISED LAMB

Korma

🍽 SERVES 4-6 🥣 WORK TIME 25-30 MINUTES ☕ COOKING TIME 2½-3 HOURS

EQUIPMENT

rolling pin without handles

chef's knife

small knife

flameproof casserole with lid

large metal spoon

metal spoon

chopping board

mortar and pestle*

Korma refers to a fragrant Indian dish in which meat is gently cooked with spices and plain yogurt. Here, the korma is made with lamb.

GETTING AHEAD

Korma can be made up to 3 days ahead and kept in the refrigerator. Add water when reheating, if necessary.

metric	SHOPPING LIST	imperial
1.4 kg	boned lamb shoulder	3 lb
6	onions, total weight about 750 g (1½ lb)	6
2.5 cm	piece of fresh root ginger	1 inch
2	garlic cloves	2
125 ml	vegetable oil	4 fl oz
250 ml	plain yogurt	8 fl oz
250 ml	double cream	8 fl oz
	salt	
3-5	sprigs of fresh coriander	3-5
	For the spice mixture	
2	dried red chillies	2
5	whole cardamom pods	5
1	cinnamon stick or 10 ml (2 tsp) ground cinnamon	1
5	whole cloves	5
7	black peppercorns	7
10 ml	ground cumin	2 tsp
5 ml	ground mace	1 tsp
5 ml	paprika	1 tsp

INGREDIENTS

boned lamb shoulder

dried red chillies

cardamom pods

cinnamon stick

black peppercorns

cloves

ground cumin

plain yogurt

double cream

onions

garlic cloves

fresh coriander

ground mace**

paprika

vegetable oil

fresh root ginger

** ground nutmeg can also be used

ORDER OF WORK

1 PREPARE THE SPICE MIXTURE AND OTHER INGREDIENTS

2 COOK THE KORMA

3 FINISH THE KORMA

* spice mill or coffee grinder can also be used

1 PREPARE THE SPICE MIXTURE AND OTHER INGREDIENTS

1 Trim and split the dried red chillies lengthwise and discard the seeds.

2 Crush the cardamom pods with the flat of the small knife, and extract the seeds with the point of the knife.

3 If using a cinnamon stick, crush it with the end of the rolling pin.

4 Put the chillies, cardamom seeds, crushed cinnamon, cloves, and peppercorns in the mortar and crush them as finely as possible with the pestle.

ANNE SAYS
"If you use a coffee grinder, wipe it well before and after grinding the spices."

Mix ground spices into freshly crushed spices

5 Stir in the cumin, mace, paprika, and ground cinnamon, if using.

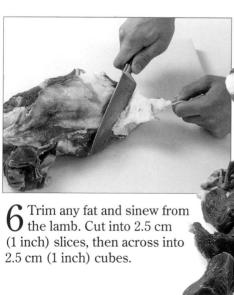

6 Trim any fat and sinew from the lamb. Cut into 2.5 cm (1 inch) slices, then across into 2.5 cm (1 inch) cubes.

Sharp chef's knife makes cubing meat easy

7 Peel the onions, leaving a little of the root attached, and cut them in half through the root and stalk. Lay each onion half on the chopping board and cut across into medium slices.

8 With the small knife, peel the skin from the ginger. With the chef's knife, slice the ginger, cutting across the fibrous grain. Crush each slice of ginger, using the flat side of the chef's knife, and finely chop the slices.

9 Set the flat side of the chef's knife on top of each garlic clove and strike it with your fist. Discard the skin and finely chop the garlic.

2 COOK THE KORMA

1 Heat the oil in the casserole. Add the onions and cook over low heat, stirring occasionally, until soft and golden brown, about 20 minutes. Stir in the ginger and garlic and cook until softened and fragrant, about 2 minutes.

Lightly frying spices develops flavour

2 Add the spice mixture and cook, stirring constantly, until thoroughly combined, 1-2 minutes. Add the lamb cubes to the casserole and cook, stirring and tossing constantly, so they absorb the flavour of the spices, about 5 minutes.

3 Add half of the yogurt, half of the double cream, and a little salt, and bring almost to a boil.

4 Reduce the heat, cover, and cook over very low heat until the lamb is tender enough to crush with your finger, 2-2½ hours. Stir occasionally during cooking so the meat does not stick. If the liquid evaporates too quickly, add a little water.

ANNE SAYS
"Fat from the sauce may separate and come to the surface during cooking. You can spoon off the fat, although traditionally it is served with the korma."

3 FINISH THE KORMA

1 Strip the coriander leaves from the stalks. Set aside a few whole leaves and pile the remainder on the chopping board. With the chef's knife, finely chop the leaves.

Use fingers to strip delicate leaves from stalks

2 Stir the remaining yogurt and double cream into the lamb. Taste for seasoning and heat until very hot. Transfer the korma to warmed plates and garnish each serving with the chopped coriander and whole coriander leaves. Serve with rice.

Fresh coriander peps up presentation

Rice topped with sultanas and toasted pine nuts is an attractive and tasty accompaniment

VARIATION

MOROCCAN SPICED LAMB

A different spice mixture gives this dish a Moroccan flavour. Serve it with couscous and harissa, the fiery Moroccan chilli sauce.

1 Substitute for the spices in the main recipe: 15 ml (1 tbsp) paprika, 10 ml (2 tsp) ground ginger, 10 ml (2 tsp) ground cumin, 5 ml (1 tsp) cayenne, and 2.5 ml (1/2 tsp) ground turmeric.

2 Prepare the lamb, onions, and 4 garlic cloves as directed; omit the fresh root ginger.

3 Mix the spices and combine with 45 g (1 1/2 oz) softened butter and the chopped garlic. Rub over the cubes of lamb. Let stand 30 minutes.

4 Cook the stew as directed, omitting the yogurt and double cream and instead adding 250 ml (8 fl oz) water to the casserole; add more water during cooking if the lamb starts to stick.

5 Meanwhile, heat the oven to 180°C (350°F, Gas 4). Spread 45 g (1 1/2 oz) flaked almonds on a baking sheet and toast in the heated oven until golden, stirring occasionally, 5-7 minutes.

6 Using a slotted spoon, transfer the lamb pieces to a serving dish or individual plates. Spoon off and discard the fat from the cooking liquid and boil until slightly thickened, 1-2 minutes. Taste for seasoning and spoon the liquid over the lamb.

7 Make a ring of couscous around the lamb. Omit the coriander and serve sprinkled with the toasted almonds.

ROAST RIB OF BEEF PEBRONATA

 SERVES 6-8 ☙ WORK TIME 25-30 MINUTES ♨ COOKING TIME 1¾-2¼ HOURS

EQUIPMENT

chef's knife

small knife

small ladle   teaspoon

slotted spoon

aluminium foil

large metal spoon   saucepan

sieve   plastic bag

metal skewer*

wooden spoon

2-pronged fork

2 frying pans   chopping board

bowls

flameproof baking dish

*meat thermometer can also be used

Many cooks choose the rib joint for roasting because the bones conduct the heat well, thus ensuring the meat will be moist. Roast rib of beef is the foundation of a grand dinner when served with Corsican pebronata sauce made with tomatoes, red peppers, garlic, red wine, and olive oil.

GETTING AHEAD

The pebronata sauce can be made 1 day in advance, kept covered in the refrigerator, and gently reheated. The beef must be roasted just before serving.

metric	SHOPPING LIST	imperial
1	beef rib roast (2 ribs), weighing about 2 kg (4½ lb)	1
	salt and pepper	
For the pebronata sauce		
1	onion	1
4	garlic cloves	4
1.4 kg	tomatoes	3 lb
3-4	sprigs of fresh thyme	3-4
3-4	sprigs of parsley	3-4
3	red peppers	3
60 ml	olive oil	4 tbsp
4	juniper berries	4
1	bay leaf	1
30 ml	plain flour	2 tbsp
500 ml	red wine	16 fl oz

INGREDIENTS

beef rib roast

parsley   fresh thyme

tomatoes

onion   plain flour

red peppers

red wine   olive oil

juniper berries

garlic cloves   bay leaf

ORDER OF WORK

1 PREPARE AND ROAST THE RIB OF BEEF

2 MAKE THE PEBRONATA SAUCE

3 FINISH THE DISH

1 PREPARE AND ROAST THE RIB OF BEEF

1 Heat the oven to 230°C (450°F, Gas 8). Trim the meat, leaving a thin layer of fat to keep it moist. Sprinkle with salt and pepper and set the meat in the baking dish with the ribs pointing upwards. Roast the meat in the heated oven until the surface starts to brown, about 15 minutes.

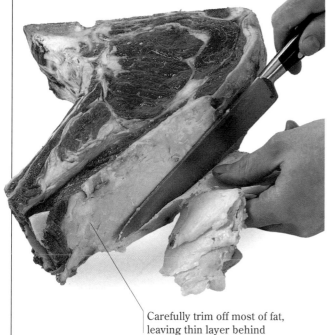

2 Reduce the oven temperature to 180°C (350°F, Gas 4). Continue roasting about 1 hour longer for rare beef, or 65-75 minutes longer for medium-done. Baste often with the juices in the dish. While the meat is roasting, make the pebronata sauce.

ANNE SAYS
"*If the meat does not produce much juice during roasting, add a few spoonfuls of water to the dish.*"

3 When the meat is rare, the skewer inserted in the centre of the meat for 30 seconds will be cool to the touch when withdrawn. If using a meat thermometer, it will show 52°C (125°F). If the meat is medium-done, the skewer will be warm. A meat thermometer will show 60°C (140°F).

Carefully trim off most of fat, leaving thin layer behind

2 MAKE THE PEBRONATA SAUCE

Finger knuckles guide blade as you chop

1 Peel the onion, leaving a little of the root attached, and cut it in half through root and stalk. Lay each onion half on the chopping board and slice horizontally towards the root, leaving the slices attached at the root end, then slice vertically, again leaving the root end uncut. Cut across the onion to make dice.

2 Set the flat side of the chef's knife on top of each garlic clove and strike it with your fist. Discard the skin and finely chop the garlic.

3 Cut the cores from the tomatoes and score an "x" on the base of each with the tip of the small knife. Immerse them in boiling water until the skin starts to split, 8-15 seconds depending on their ripeness. Using the slotted spoon, transfer them at once to a bowl of cold water.

4 When the tomatoes are cold, peel off the skin. Cut the tomatoes crosswise in half and squeeze out the seeds, then finely chop.

Skin is easy to peel off after tomatoes have been blanched

5 Strip the thyme and parsley leaves from the stalks and pile them on the chopping board. With the chef's knife, coarsely chop the leaves.

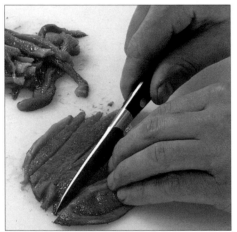

6 Roast, peel, and core the red peppers (see box, page 85). Cut each half lengthwise into thin strips.

7 Heat half of the oil in one frying pan; add the onion. Sauté, stirring, 3-4 minutes. Add the garlic, thyme, and parsley and sauté 1 minute. Stir in the tomatoes, salt, and pepper and cook, stirring often, until most of the liquid has evaporated, about 25 minutes.

8 Meanwhile, put the juniper berries on the chopping board, set the flat side of the chef's knife on top, and strike the knife blade with your fist to crush the berries.

Crush juniper berries with sharp blow of fist on flat side of knife

9 Heat the remaining oil in the second frying pan, add the red pepper strips, bay leaf, and juniper berries, and cook, stirring occasionally, until the peppers are soft, 8-10 minutes.

10 Sprinkle the flour over the peppers and cook, stirring, until lightly browned, 1-2 minutes.

Flour acts as thickener for sauce

Use wooden spoon to combine tomato and pepper mixtures

12 Stir in the onion and tomato mixture and simmer until it is quite thick, 8-10 minutes. Discard the bay leaf and taste the sauce for seasoning.

11 Stir in half of the red wine and bring to a boil, stirring until the mixture thickens. Simmer 2 minutes.

HOW TO ROAST, PEEL, AND CORE PEPPERS

After they are roasted, peeled, and cored, peppers can be stuffed whole, sliced and added to salads, or cooked alone or with other vegetables.

1 Heat the grill; set the peppers on a rack 10 cm (4 inches) from the heat. Grill, turning once or twice, until black and blistered, 10-12 minutes. Wrap in a plastic bag to trap steam and loosen the skin. Let cool.

2 With a small knife, peel off the skin from each pepper, and rinse the peppers under running water. Pat them dry with paper towels.

3 Cut out the cores. If the peppers are not to be used whole for stuffing, they are easier to deseed if first cut lengthwise in half. Scrape out the seeds with a teaspoon.

3 FINISH THE DISH

1 When the meat is cooked to your taste, transfer it to a board, cover it loosely with foil, and leave in a warm place, 10-15 minutes.

2 Tilt the baking dish and spoon off the fat with the large metal spoon. Discard the fat.

ANNE SAYS
"Letting the meat stand allows the juices to redistribute evenly throughout the meat, making it easier to carve."

Wrapping of foil keeps beef warm while gravy is made

3 Add the remaining red wine to the baking dish. Bring to the boil, stirring to dissolve the juices in the dish. Simmer 2-3 minutes.

Bundles of green beans and carrots are tied with blanched strips of spring onion

4 Strain into the pebronata sauce. Taste again for seasoning.

🍽 **TO SERVE**
Carve the beef (see box, page 87), arrange slices on warmed plates, and, if you like, spoon over the juices from the carving board. Add sauce to each plate and pass the remainder separately.

Pebronata sauce brings taste of Mediterranean

V A R I A T I O N

ROAST RIB OF BEEF WITH YORKSHIRE PUDDING

Traditional Sunday lunch: roast rib of beef served with crisp and golden Yorkshire puddings.

1 Roast the beef as directed, in a roasting tin.

2 Meanwhile, make the batter: sift 180 g (6 oz) plain flour into a large bowl. Make a well in the centre and add 2 beaten eggs with salt and pepper. Slowly whisk in 300 ml (½ pint) milk, drawing in the flour to form a smooth paste. Stir in 90 ml (3 fl oz) water. Cover and let stand at least 15 minutes.

3 When the meat is done, transfer it to a board and cover loosely with foil.

4 Increase the oven heat to 230° C (450° F, Gas 8). Remove the fat from the roasting tin. Pour a teaspoon into each of 12 deep bun tins, adding vegetable oil if necessary, and heat in the oven until very hot, 5 minutes.

5 Pour in the batter to half-fill the tins. Bake in the hot oven until puffed and very brown, 15-20 minutes.

6 Meanwhile, make the gravy: stir 15-30 ml (1-2 tbsp) plain flour into the juices in the roasting tin and cook, stirring, until very brown, 2-3 minutes. Add 500 ml (16 fl oz) beef or brown veal stock or water. Bring to a boil, stirring; simmer 2 minutes. Strain and season to taste.

7 Carve the joint and arrange on warmed plates with the Yorkshire puddings and vegetables of your choice. Serve the gravy separately.

HOW TO CARVE A RIB ROAST

1 Set the joint upright on a carving board and, holding it steady with a 2-pronged fork, cut away the rib bones at the base of the meat to facilitate carving.

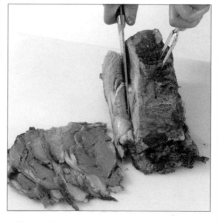

2 With the joint on its side and the knife at a slight angle, carve into 2 cm (¾ inch) slices.

V A R I A T I O N

ROAST RIB OF BEEF WITH GLAZED ONIONS, TURNIPS, AND CARROTS

As an accompaniment for roast rib of beef, glazed vegetables are an ideal winter alternative to pebronata sauce.

1 Roast the beef as directed, in a roasting tin.

2 Meanwhile, put 15 pickling onions (total weight about 250 g/8 oz) in a bowl, pour over hot water to cover, and let stand 2 minutes to loosen the skins. Drain the onions and peel with a small knife.

3 Trim the ends from 250 g (8 oz) small turnips and cut them lengthwise into quarters. Using a small knife, round the sharp edges of the turnip quarters and peel away the skin.

4 Peel and trim 250 g (8 oz) carrots and cut into 5 cm (2 inch) lengths. Cut broader pieces into halves or quarters. Round the edges as for the turnips.

5 Put each of the vegetables in a separate small pan and add 15 g (½ oz) butter and 10 ml (2 tsp) granulated sugar to each, with just enough water barely to cover. Season with salt and pepper. Bring to a boil and simmer until the liquid has almost evaporated, 8-10 minutes for the pickling onions, 12-15 minutes for the carrots, and 8-10 minutes for the turnips. If the vegetables are not tender when the water has evaporated, add 30-45 ml (2-3 tbsp) more water and continue cooking. Shake the vegetables in the pan from time to time so they are evenly coated with glaze.

6 Transfer the beef to a board, cover with foil, and let stand 10-15 minutes. Dissolve the juices from the roasting tin in red wine as directed. Add an equal quantity of beef or brown veal stock or water and bring to a boil. Taste the gravy for seasoning, then strain.

7 Carve the joint, arrange the slices on warmed plates, and garnish with the glazed vegetables. Spoon over a little gravy and decorate with fresh herb sprigs. Serve the remaining gravy separately.

PROVENÇAL BEEF STEW

Daube de Boeuf aux Olives Noires

🍽 SERVES 6-8　🥣 WORK TIME 45-50 MINUTES*　🍲 COOKING TIME 3½-4 HOURS

EQUIPMENT

chef's knife

small knife

flameproof casserole with lid

vegetable peeler

saucepans

wooden spoon

fork

colander

slotted spoon

sieve

olive stoner

scissors

kitchen string

bowls

small plate

paper towels

muslin

large plate

chopping board

Here cubes of beef are marinated with plenty of herbs and flavourings, and then simmered until tender in red wine. The colour of the finished stew is rich and the aroma intense and appetizing.

* *plus 24-48 hours marinating time*

metric	SHOPPING LIST	imperial
1 kg	braising steak	2 lb
250 g	piece of smoked streaky bacon, or rashers	8 oz
250 g	piece of lean salt pork, or more bacon	8 oz
2	carrots	2
2	onions	2
500 g	medium tomatoes	1 lb
175 g	mushrooms	6 oz
200 g	unstoned black olives	6½ oz
	salt and pepper	
250 ml	beef or brown veal stock (see box, page 36) or water, more if needed	8 fl oz
45 g	butter	1½ oz
45 ml	plain flour	3 tbsp
For the marinade		
1	orange	1
2	garlic cloves	2
500 ml	red wine	16 fl oz
2	bay leaves	2
3-4	sprigs each of fresh rosemary, thyme, and parsley	3-4
10	peppercorns	10
30 ml	olive oil	2 tbsp

INGREDIENTS

streaky bacon

carrots

braising steak

tomatoes

onions　mushrooms

salt pork

butter　beef stock

black olives

plain flour

parsley

fresh rosemary

orange

olive oil

red wine

fresh thyme

garlic　peppercorns

bay leaves

ORDER OF WORK

1 MARINATE THE BEEF

2 PREPARE THE STEW

3 COOK THE STEW

4 FINISH THE DISH

1 MARINATE THE BEEF

1 Cut the beef into 4 cm (1½ inch) strips, then across into 4 cm (1½ inch) cubes; trim off excess fat.

Use chef's knife to cut and trim meat

2 Peel the zest from the orange in wide strips. Set the flat side of the chef's knife on top of the garlic cloves and strike it with your fist. Discard the skin and finely chop the garlic.

Use your hands to mix beef cubes with marinade ingredients to ensure meat is evenly coated

3 Combine the orange zest, garlic, red wine, bay leaves, rosemary, thyme, parsley, and peppercorns in a non-metallic bowl. Add the beef and mix well. Pour the olive oil on top. Cover tightly and let marinate in the refrigerator, turning the beef occasionally, 24-48 hours.

ANNE SAYS
"Oil keeps the meat from drying out."

HOW TO SLICE ONIONS

Onions can be cut into thick or thin slices to use in many dishes.

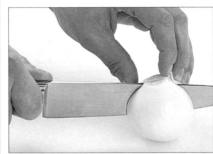

1 Peel the onion, leaving a little of the root attached, and cut it in half through root and stalk.

2 Lay each half on the chopping board and cut across into thin or thick slices, as required.

2 PREPARE THE STEW

1 Cut the bacon into 5 mm (¼ inch) thick rashers, if necessary, discarding any rind. Stack and cut into 5 mm (¼ inch) wide strips. Cut the salt pork into dice or strips.

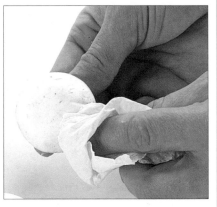

Dice salt pork and discard any excess fat

2 Put the bacon and salt pork in a saucepan of cold water, heat to boiling, and blanch 10 minutes. Drain in the colander, rinse with cold water, and drain again thoroughly.

ANNE SAYS
"This blanching removes excess salt."

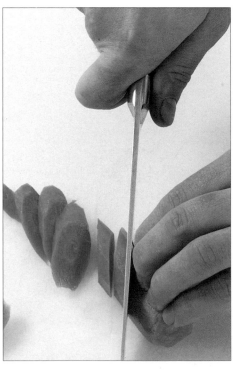

3 Peel and trim the carrots and cut them diagonally into 1 cm (½ inch) slices with the chef's knife. Peel and slice the onions (see box, page 89).

HOW TO CLEAN AND SLICE MUSHROOMS

Mushrooms absorb moisture quickly, so do not soak them in water. In order to cook evenly, mushrooms should be cut into equal-sized pieces.

1 Wipe the mushroom caps with a damp paper towel.

2 Trim the mushroom stalks even with the caps.

3 Set the mushrooms stalk-side down on a chopping board and slice them.

Using olive stoner saves time

Stoned olives are left with neat cavity

4 Score an "x" on the base of each tomato. Immerse the tomatoes in boiling water until the skin starts to split. Transfer them at once to cold water. When cold, peel off the skin. Cut the tomatoes crosswise in half and squeeze out the seeds, then chop each half coarsely.

5 Clean and slice the mushrooms (see box, page 90). Stone the olives.

COOK THE STEW

1 Heat the oven to 150°C (300°F, Gas 2). Remove the beef pieces from the marinade, place on paper towels on the large plate, and pat dry; set aside.

2 Strain the marinade. Reserve the liquid and tie the flavouring ingredients in a piece of muslin.

Absorption of marinade darkens meat

Strain to separate marinade flavourings from liquid

3 Spread the bacon and salt pork on the bottom of the casserole and cover with the beef cubes. Layer the tomatoes and onions on top.

Layer vegetables on top of meat

4 Continue layering with the carrots, mushrooms, and black olives. Pour in the strained marinade and the stock and season with pepper. Add the bag of flavourings.

! TAKE CARE !
The bacon, salt pork, and olives will add salt so more may not be needed.

5 Bring the stew slowly to a boil on top of the stove, then cover the casserole, transfer to the heated oven, and cook 3½-4 hours, stirring occasionally.

Tender meat is easily crushed in fingers

6 The beef is ready when it is tender enough to crush in your fingers. Add more stock if the stew seems dry.

4 FINISH THE DISH

1 Make beurre manié (kneaded butter): using the fork, crush the butter on the small plate. Work in the flour until smooth.

2 Transfer the casserole to the top of the stove and discard the flavouring bag. Add the beurre manié in small pieces, stirring so it melts into the sauce and thickens it. Simmer 2 minutes; taste for seasoning. Serve in warmed dishes or bowls. Decorate with rosemary sprigs, if you like.

Black olives star in this succulent stew

Tender beef is ready to melt in your mouth

VARIATION

PROVENÇAL LAMB STEW WITH GREEN OLIVES

Here, more traditional lamb replaces the beef, and green olives are substituted for black olives.

1 Cut 1 kg (2 lb) boned lamb shoulder into cubes, using a chef's knife.
2 Marinate the cubes of lamb 24-48 hours as directed.
3 Prepare the bacon, salt pork, and vegetables as directed, stoning green olives instead of black.
4 Cook the stew as directed.
5 Make the beurre manié and finish the dish as directed, sprinkling a little chopped thyme on each serving, if you like.

GETTING AHEAD

The stew can be made up to 2 days ahead and kept, covered, in the refrigerator. Reheat on top of the stove until bubbling.

CHILLI CON CARNE

 SERVES 6   WORK TIME 35-40 MINUTES   COOKING TIME 2-2½ HOURS

EQUIPMENT

large heavy casserole with lid

plate

small knife

chef's knife

saucepan

wooden spoon

slotted spoon

bowls

chopping board

ladle

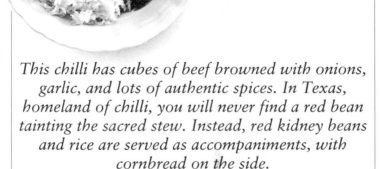

This chilli has cubes of beef browned with onions, garlic, and lots of authentic spices. In Texas, homeland of chilli, you will never find a red bean tainting the sacred stew. Instead, red kidney beans and rice are served as accompaniments, with cornbread on the side.

GETTING AHEAD
Chilli can be refrigerated up to 3 days and the flavour will mellow. It can also be frozen.

INGREDIENTS

braising steak

fresh oregano

vegetable oil

tomatoes

onions

dried red chillies

paprika

chilli powder

fine cornmeal

Tabasco sauce

garlic cloves

ground cumin

metric	SHOPPING LIST	imperial
3	medium onions	3
3	garlic cloves	3
750 g	tomatoes	1½ lb
2-4	dried red chillies	2-4
5-6	sprigs of fresh oregano or 15 ml (1 tbsp) dried	5-6
1.4 kg	braising steak	3 lb
45 ml	vegetable oil, more if needed	3 tbsp
500 ml	water, more if needed	16 fl oz
30 ml	chilli powder	2 tbsp
15 ml	paprika	1 tbsp
10 ml	ground cumin	2 tsp
5-10 ml	Tabasco sauce, or to taste	1-2 tsp
	salt and pepper	
15 ml	fine cornmeal (polenta)	1 tbsp

ORDER OF WORK

1 **PREPARE CHILLI INGREDIENTS**

2 **COOK THE CHILLI**

1 PREPARE THE CHILLI INGREDIENTS

1 Peel the onions, leaving a little of the root attached, and cut in half through root and stalk. Slice each half horizontally towards the root, leaving the slices attached at the root end, then slice vertically, again leaving the root end uncut. Cut across to make dice.

2 Set the flat side of the chef's knife on top of each garlic clove and strike it with your fist. Discard the skin and finely chop the garlic. Peel, deseed, and finely chop the tomatoes (see box, page 96).

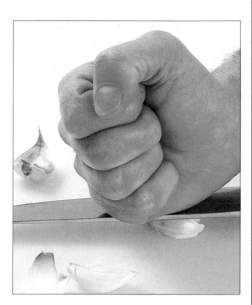

3 Trim and split the chillies lengthwise. Discard the seeds, then finely chop or crumble them. If using fresh oregano, strip the leaves from the stalks, put in a pile, and chop.

ANNE SAYS
"The seeds are the hottest part of dried red chillies; if you like your chilli extra hot you can leave them in."

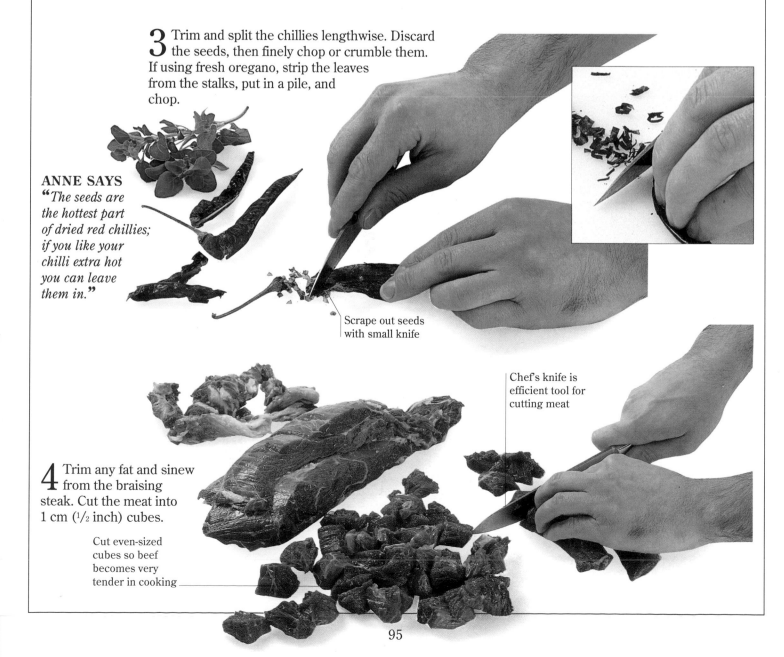

Scrape out seeds with small knife

Chef's knife is efficient tool for cutting meat

4 Trim any fat and sinew from the braising steak. Cut the meat into 1 cm (¹/₂ inch) cubes.

Cut even-sized cubes so beef becomes very tender in cooking

2 COOK THE CHILLI

Browning meat adds flavour to chilli

1 Heat half of the oil in the casserole, add about one-quarter of the beef cubes, and cook over high heat, stirring, until browned. Using the slotted spoon, transfer the meat to the plate. Brown the remaining beef cubes in 3 batches, adding more oil as needed.

! TAKE CARE !
It is important to cook the beef cubes in batches so that they brown quickly without giving off much liquid.

2 Return the 3 batches of browned meat, with the juices, to the final batch of meat in the casserole. Add the onions, garlic, and tomatoes and cook, stirring, until the onions are just soft, 8-10 minutes.

HOW TO PEEL, DESEED, AND CHOP TOMATOES

Tomatoes are often peeled and deseeded before they are chopped so they can be cooked to form a smooth purée.

1 Fill a small saucepan with water and bring to a boil. Using a small knife, cut out the core and stalk from each tomato.

2 Turn the tomatoes over and score an "x" on the base of each with the tip of the knife.

3 Immerse the tomatoes in the pan of water until the skin starts to split, 8-15 seconds. Transfer them at once to a bowl of cold water.

Use knife and finger to peel off skin

4 When the tomatoes are cold, peel off the skin from each.

5 Cut the tomatoes crosswise in half and squeeze out the seeds, loosening them with your finger.

6 Set each half cut-side down and slice. Turn the slices 90° and slice again. Chop the tomato flesh coarsely or finely, as needed.

3 Pour in the water, and stir into the casserole with the chillies, oregano, chilli powder, paprika, cumin, Tabasco sauce, salt, and pepper. Bring just to a boil, then cover the casserole, and simmer until the meat is very tender, about 2-2½ hours, stirring occasionally.

Chilli powder gives zing to dish

Cornmeal thickens chilli and adds flavour

4 About 30 minutes before the end of cooking, stir in the cornmeal. At the end of cooking, the chilli should be thick and rich.

Red kidney beans are traditionally served separately, but some cooks mix them into the chili

🍴 **TO SERVE**
Taste the chilli for seasoning, and serve it hot from the casserole, with boiled white long-grain rice, squares of cornbread (see pages 108-109), and bowls of red kidney beans.

(see pages 108-109)

Meat is tender, juicy, and spicy

MEXICAN CHILLI CON CARNE

This variation goes "south of the border", adding plain chocolate and extra spice to the sauce, to create a Mexican "mole".

1 Prepare the onions, garlic, tomatoes, dried red chillies, and beef as directed; omit the oregano.
2 Brown the meat, then cook with the onions, garlic, chillies, and tomatoes as directed.
3 Add the water, ground spices, and Tabasco with 30 g (1 oz) chopped plain chocolate, 5 ml (1 tsp) ground cloves, and 10 ml (2 tsp) ground cinnamon. Finish as directed.
4 If you like, mix the red kidney beans into the chilli, and accompany with slices of avocado and tortilla chips.

BURGUNDY POT ROAST

Boeuf à la Bourguignonne

 SERVES 6-8   WORK TIME 25-30 MINUTES   COOKING TIME 3½-4 HOURS

EQUIPMENT

chef's knife

small knife

slotted spoon

large metal spoon

kitchen string   kitchen scissors

small ladle

2-pronged fork   vegetable peeler

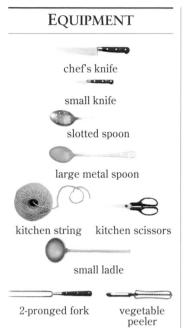

flameproof casserole with lid

sieve

frying pan

plate

colander   bowls

paper towels

Few French dishes are better known than this traditional dish from Burgundy. The secret of a successful pot roast is well-aged beef and a hearty red wine, such as Pinot Noir, to add substance. The classic Burgundian garnish of bacon, red wine, small whole onions, and mushrooms is delicious with a beef pot roast.

GETTING AHEAD

Burgundy Pot Roast can be made up to 3 days ahead and kept, covered, in the refrigerator; the flavour improves on standing. Reheat it on top of the stove until bubbling.

metric	SHOPPING LIST	imperial
1	onion	1
2	whole cloves	2
1	carrot	1
45 ml	vegetable oil	3 tbsp
1	beef topside, weighing 1.4-1.6 kg (3-3½ lb)	1
1	bouquet garni, made with 5-6 parsley stalks, 2-3 fresh thyme sprigs, and 1 bay leaf	1
250 ml	red wine	8 fl oz
	salt and pepper	
250 ml	beef stock (see box, page 36), more if needed	8 fl oz
16-20	pickling onions	16-20
250 g	mushrooms	8 oz
250 g	piece of smoked streaky bacon, or rashers	8 oz

INGREDIENTS

beef topside

streaky bacon   beef stock

onion   pickling onions

carrot

mushrooms

bouquet garni   cloves

red wine   vegetable oil

ORDER OF WORK

1 COOK THE POT ROAST

2 PREPARE THE GARNISH

3 FINISH THE DISH

1 COOK THE POT ROAST

1 Heat the oven to 170°C (325°F, Gas 3). Peel the onion and stud with the cloves. Peel and quarter the carrot.

2 If necessary, roll the beef topside into a neat shape and, using separate pieces of string, tie the roast at 2.5 cm (1 inch) intervals to hold the shape.

Browning seals juices into meat

3 Heat 30 ml (2 tbsp) of the oil in the casserole. Add the meat and brown it well on all sides, turning it with the 2-pronged fork.

! TAKE CARE !
The oil must be very hot to sear the meat and seal in the juices.

4 Remove the casserole from the heat, take out the meat, and discard all but 30 ml (2 tbsp) of fat from the casserole.

5 Replace the meat in the casserole, and add the clove-studded onion, carrot, bouquet garni, red wine, salt, and pepper. Cover and cook the pot roast in the heated oven 30 minutes.

ANNE SAYS
"Do not add too much salt because the bacon garnish will be salty."

6 Pour in the beef stock and stir well to mix with the liquid in the casserole.

Fork easily pierces fully cooked pot roast

7 Turn the meat 3 or 4 times during cooking, using the 2-pronged fork, and add more stock if too much liquid evaporates. Continue cooking the beef about 3 hours. Meanwhile, prepare the garnish.

2 PREPARE THE GARNISH

1 Put the pickling onions in a bowl, pour over hot water to cover the onions, and let stand 2 minutes.

Little onions are easy to peel after blanching in boiling water

2 Drain the onions in the colander, and peel them with the small knife.

3 Wipe the mushroom caps with a damp paper towel and trim the stalks even with the caps. Set the mushrooms stalk-side down on the chopping board and slice them.

4 Cut the bacon into 5 mm (¼ inch) thick rashers, if necessary, discarding any rind. Stack and cut into 5 mm (¼ inch) strips. Heat the remaining oil in a frying pan.

5 Add the bacon to the pan and fry until browned and the fat is rendered (melted down), 3-5 minutes. Transfer to a bowl.

6 Add the pickling onions to the pan and cook, stirring occasionally, until lightly browned, 3-5 minutes. Add to the bacon using the slotted spoon.

7 Add the mushrooms to the frying pan and cook, stirring occasionally, until tender, 2-3 minutes. Transfer them to the bowl containing the bacon and onions.

All liquid should be evaporated when cooking mushrooms

3 FINISH THE DISH

1 Remove the meat from the casserole. Strain the cooking liquid, discarding the flavourings. If the liquid is too thin, return it to the casserole and boil until reduced and slightly thickened. Return the meat to the casserole with the cooking liquid, and add the bacon, pickling onions, and mushrooms. Cover and continue cooking 30 minutes, or until very tender.

2 Transfer the meat to the chopping board. Skim any fat from the cooking liquid and taste for seasoning. Remove and discard the string from the beef, then cut into 12 thick slices.

🍴 TO SERVE

Arrange the slices of beef on warmed plates. Spoon the garnish and a little of the cooking liquid over the meat. Serve the remainder separately. Decorate each plate with fresh thyme sprigs, if you like.

Bacon garnish introduces piquant note

VARIATION

FLEMISH POT ROAST WITH BEER

This classic Flemish dish uses beer and lots of sliced onions in place of red wine and the Burgundian garnish. Accompany with braised red cabbage sprinkled with chopped herbs.

1 Peel 6 onions (total weight about 750 g/1½ lb), leaving a little of the root attached, and cut them in half through root and stalk. Lay each onion half on the chopping board and cut across into thick slices.

2 Peel and trim 2 carrots, and cut crosswise into 2.5 cm (1 inch) pieces. Cut each piece lengthwise into 5 mm (¼ inch) slices. Stack the slices and cut into 5 mm (¼ inch) sticks.

3 Brown the beef as directed. Remove the beef and cook the onions in the casserole over very low heat, stirring occasionally, until soft and lightly browned, 20-30 minutes.

4 Return the beef to the casserole and add the carrots. Continue cooking as directed, omitting the clove-studded onion and carrot for flavouring, using beer in place of the red wine, and adding a pinch of ground nutmeg.

5 Omit the bacon, pickling onion, and mushroom garnish.

6 Finish as directed, without straining the cooking liquid, but discarding the bouquet garni.

FRENCH HOT POT

Pot-au-Feu

🍽 SERVES 8　⚒ WORK TIME 40-45 MINUTES　🍲 COOKING TIME 3½-4 HOURS

EQUIPMENT

chef's knife

small knife

slotted spoon

2-pronged fork

ladle

saucepan

sieve

kitchen scissors

vegetable peeler

kitchen string

serrated knife

aluminium foil

palette knife

teaspoon

knife

bowls

muslin

flameproof casserole

baking sheet

chopping board

In this time-honoured French country dish, beef is simmered with aromatic vegetables to spoon-cutting tenderness. The recipe forms two courses: the rich cooking broth is followed by the meat and vegetables, although you can serve them together. Gherkins, sea salt, and mustard are the classic accompaniments.

GETTING AHEAD

The hot pot can be made up to 2 days ahead and kept, covered, in the refrigerator. Reheat until bubbling on top of the stove.

metric	SHOPPING LIST	imperial
1 kg	boneless beef shin	2 lb
1	onion	1
2	whole cloves	2
1.4 kg	beef blade steak	3 lb
4 litres	white veal stock (see box, page 36) or water, more if needed	7 pints
1	large bouquet garni	1
	salt	
10	peppercorns	10
500 g	carrots	1 lb
1	small head of celery	1
750 g	leeks	1½ lb
1 kg	marrow bones	2 lb
125 g	loaf of French bread	4 oz

INGREDIENTS

boneless beef shin*

beef blade steak

peppercorns

onion

leeks

marrow bones

bouquet garni

carrots

celery

French bread

white veal stock

whole cloves

*brisket can also be used

ORDER OF WORK

1 START COOKING THE BEEF

2 PREPARE AND ADD THE VEGETABLES AND MARROW

3 FINISH THE HOT POT

1 START COOKING THE BEEF

Tie meat securely so it will hold its shape

1 Tie a piece of string lengthwise around the beef shin. Using separate pieces of string, tie the beef at 2.5 cm (1 inch) intervals to form a neat cylinder of meat.

ANNE SAYS
"Tying the meat stops it from curling during cooking."

2 Peel the onion and stud it with the cloves.

3 Put the shin, blade steak, and stock in the casserole. Bring to a boil, skimming. Add the onion, the bouquet garni, made with 12-15 parsley stalks, 4-5 sprigs of fresh thyme, and 2 bay leaves (see box, below), salt, and peppercorns. Simmer gently, uncovered, 2 hours. Skim occasionally.

HOW TO MAKE A BOUQUET GARNI

This bundle of aromatic flavouring herbs is designed to be easily lifted from the casserole and discarded at the end of cooking.

To make a bouquet garni, hold together the number of parsley stalks, sprigs of fresh thyme, and bay leaves required by the recipe. Wind a piece of string around the herbs and tie securely, leaving a length of string to tie to the casserole handle, if necessary.

Hold herbs firmly together and tie into neat bouquet with string

2 PREPARE AND ADD THE VEGETABLES AND MARROW

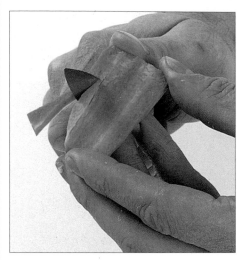

1 Peel and trim the carrots, then cut into 7.5 cm (3 inch) lengths. Cut each piece lengthwise in half. Using the small knife, trim the sharp edges to make rounded, barrel shapes.

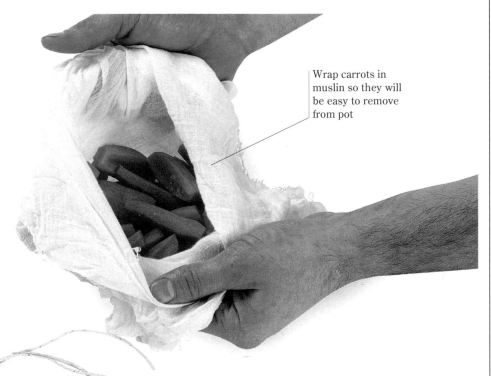

Wrap carrots in muslin so they will be easy to remove from pot

Use string to secure vegetable parcel

2 Put the carrots on a piece of muslin, gather up the ends of the cloth, and tie them securely with string to form a parcel, so that the carrots will be easy to remove at the end of cooking.

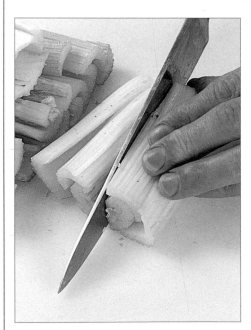

3 Trim the base and leaves from the celery, if necessary. Cut the sticks into 7.5 cm (3 inch) lengths and the heart into quarters. Put the celery in muslin and tie with string.

Hold leek leaves apart to rinse out any grit

4 Trim the leeks, discarding the roots and tough green tops. Slit the leeks lengthwise in half and wash them thoroughly under running water.

5 Cut the leek halves into 7.5 cm (3 inch) lengths, put them in muslin, and tie with string.

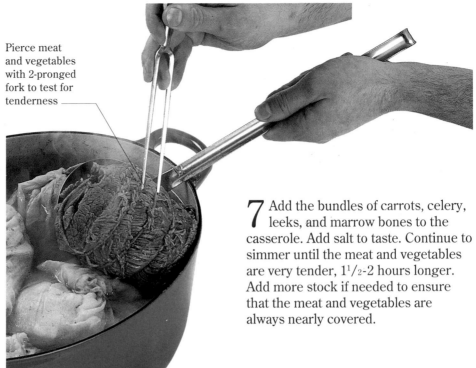

Pierce meat and vegetables with 2-pronged fork to test for tenderness

6 Put the marrow bones on a piece of muslin, gather up the ends, and tie securely with string.

ANNE SAYS
"The muslin parcel stops the marrow from falling out during cooking."

7 Add the bundles of carrots, celery, leeks, and marrow bones to the casserole. Add salt to taste. Continue to simmer until the meat and vegetables are very tender, 1^1/$_2$-2 hours longer. Add more stock if needed to ensure that the meat and vegetables are always nearly covered.

3 FINISH THE HOT POT

1 Heat the oven to 180°C (350°F, Gas 4). Cut the bread diagonally into about 20 slices. Arrange the slices on the baking sheet and toast in the heated oven, turning once, until brown around the edges, about 10 minutes.

Turn slices with palette knife so they brown evenly

2 Transfer the meat and marrow bones to the chopping board, cover with foil, and keep warm. Remove the bundles of vegetables from the broth.

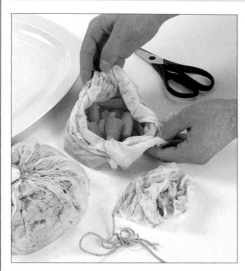

3 Unwrap the bundles of vegetables. Arrange the carrots, celery, and leeks around the edge of a warmed platter, cover with foil, and keep hot.

Reduced broth is pale golden and full of flavour

4 Taste the broth for seasoning and, if necessary, boil it until it is reduced and well flavoured.

5 Strain the broth into the saucepan and skim off any fat with the slotted spoon.

6 Discard the strings from the beef shin and cut it into generous slices. Cut the blade steak into pieces, discarding any bones that fall out. Overlap the slices of beef in the centre of the platter with the blade steak pieces alongside, so they are framed by the vegetables. Cover and keep warm.

7 Untie and unwrap the marrow bones, and scoop out the marrow from the bones with the teaspoon.

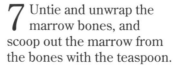

8 Spread each of the toasted slices of French bread with a little of the marrow.

Marrow adds savour to toast

Marrow-topped toast is rich and satisfying in full-flavoured broth

🍽 **TO SERVE**
Put the toasts in soup bowls, pour over the hot broth, and serve immediately as a first course. Serve the beef and vegetables as a main course.

Pot-au-feu is a warming winter meal

V A R I A T I O N

POTEE

Another French classic, this variation of Pot-au-Feu uses pork instead of beef.

1 Tie up a 1.4 kg (3 lb) rolled pork shoulder into a neat bundle. Put it in a casserole with a 500 g (1 lb) piece of smoked bacon, the stock or water, clove-studded onion, bouquet garni, salt, and peppercorns, and simmer as directed.

2 Trim the outer leaves from 1 head of cabbage (weighing about 1 kg/2 lb), and cut the cabbage into 6 wedges. Half-fill a large saucepan with water, bring to a boil, and add salt and the cabbage wedges. Blanch 5 minutes; drain, rinse the wedges with cold water, and drain again thoroughly.

3 Omit the marrow bones. Tie the carrots, celery, and leeks in separate pieces of muslin. Add to the broth with the cabbage and finish as directed, cutting the core from the cabbage wedges before serving.

4 Serve the broth with the toasted bread as a first course. Follow with individual servings of pork and bacon accompanied by the vegetables and remaining broth.

PORK NOISETTES WITH CORNBREAD AND CRANBERRIES

🍽 SERVES 4　🥣 WORK TIME 35-45 MINUTES　🍲 COOKING TIME 1-1¼ HOURS*

EQUIPMENT

chef's knife

teaspoon

vegetable peeler

wooden cocktail sticks

food processor**

bowls

large frying pan

flameproof casserole with lid

plate

small saucepan

20 cm (8 inch) square cake tin

wooden spoon

slotted spoon

sieve

whisk

2-pronged fork

boning knife

wire rack

pastry brush

metal skewer

**blender can also be used

A stuffing of cornbread with crunchy pecan nuts and celery contrasts well with the firm meat of pork, while a cranberry sauce adds a nice balance of tartness. Noisettes are cut from the boned loin and must be very thick to hold the stuffing.

*plus 20-25 minutes baking time for cornbread

metric	SHOPPING LIST	imperial
1	large onion	1
90 g	pecan nut halves	3 oz
1	celery stick	1
60 g	butter	2 oz
	salt and pepper	
1 kg	boned pork loin joint	2 lb
30 ml	vegetable oil	2 tbsp
250 ml	white wine	8 fl oz
180 g	fresh or defrosted cranberries	6 oz
30-45 ml	caster sugar	2-3 tbsp
For the cornbread		
60 g	butter, more for cake tin	2 oz
150 g	fine cornmeal (polenta)	5 oz
125 g	plain flour	4 oz
15 ml	caster sugar	1 tbsp
15 ml	baking powder	1 tbsp
250 ml	milk	8 fl oz
2	eggs	2

INGREDIENTS

cranberries

boned pork loin

celery

fine cornmeal

plain flour

vegetable oil

milk

onion

butter

pecan nuts

eggs

white wine

baking powder

caster sugar

ORDER OF WORK

1 MAKE THE CORNBREAD

2 MAKE THE STUFFING

3 STUFF AND COOK THE PORK

4 MAKE THE CRANBERRY SAUCE

1 MAKE THE CORNBREAD

Pour mixture into centre of tin to allow it to spread evenly

1 Heat the oven to 220°C (425°F, Gas 7). Butter the cake tin. Melt the butter. Sift the cornmeal, flour, sugar, 5 ml (1 tsp) salt, and the baking powder into a medium bowl and make a well in the centre.

2 Whisk the milk and eggs in a small bowl until combined. Pour them into the well in the dry ingredients and add the melted butter. Mix gently with the wooden spoon until combined.

3 Pour the mixture into the tin and bake until the skewer inserted in the centre comes out clean, 20-25 minutes. Let cool; cut into 9 squares.

2 MAKE THE STUFFING

Cornbread crumbs help to bind stuffing

1 Work 2 cornbread squares in the food processor to form crumbs. Reserve the remaining cornbread squares for serving.

2 Peel and chop the onion. Chop the pecan nuts coarsely. Peel the strings from the celery stick with the vegetable peeler and cut into thin slices.

3 Heat 45 g (1½ oz) of butter in the frying pan, add the onion and celery, and cook, stirring, until soft but not brown, 5-7 minutes. Take from the heat, add three-quarters of the pecan nuts, the cornbread crumbs, salt, and pepper, and stir to combine.

3 STUFF AND COOK THE PORK

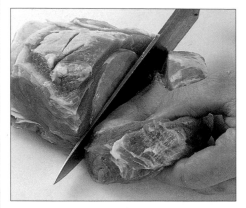

1 Heat the oven to 180°C (350°F, Gas 4). Trim any sinew and excess fat from the loin of pork. Cut across into four 4 cm (1½ inch) noisettes.

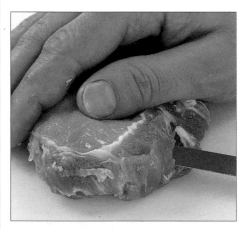

Teaspoon is just right size to insert stuffing into pocket in noisette

2 Using the boning knife, make a deep slit in the side of each noisette to form a pocket. Season the noisettes inside and out.

3 Spoon the stuffing into each pocket, packing it in well. Secure the opening in each noisette with a cocktail stick.

4 Heat the oil and remaining 15 g (½ oz) butter in the casserole. Add 2 noisettes. Brown thoroughly on one side, 3-5 minutes. Turn the noisettes over and brown on the other side, 3-5 minutes. Transfer them to the plate with the slotted spoon and brown the remaining 2 noisettes. Return the first 2 noisettes to the casserole.

5 Pour in enough water to come halfway up the noisettes. Cover and cook in the heated oven, turning once, 1-1¼ hours. If the casserole gets dry, add a little more water. The noisettes are cooked if they are tender when pierced with the 2-pronged fork.

! TAKE CARE !
Do not overcook the pork noisettes or they will be tough and dry.

6 Transfer the noisettes to a warmed serving platter or individual plates, using the slotted spoon. Remove the cocktail sticks from the noisettes, cover the meat, and keep it warm while you make the cranberry sauce.

4 MAKE THE CRANBERRY SAUCE

1 Skim off and discard any excess fat from the casserole; heat the juices to boiling. Boil until reduced by half. Add the wine, cranberries, sugar, salt, and pepper. Bring to a boil and cook, stirring occasionally, until the cranberries pop and are tender, 8-12 minutes.

Add cranberries to reduced cooking juices and wine

🍽 TO SERVE

Sprinkle the noisettes with the remaining chopped pecan nuts. Serve the reserved cornbread, cut into triangles, on the side, and the cranberry sauce separately. Decorate with celery leaves.

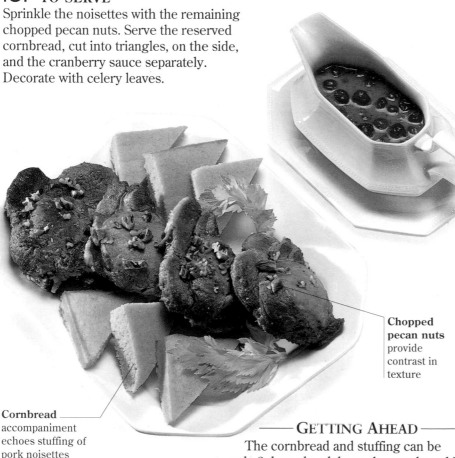

Chopped pecan nuts provide contrast in texture

Cornbread accompaniment echoes stuffing of pork noisettes

GETTING AHEAD

The cornbread and stuffing can be made 2 days ahead; keep the cornbread in an airtight container; cover the stuffing and refrigerate. Stuff the noisettes not more than 4 hours ahead; cook just before serving.

VARIATION

PORK NOISETTES WITH CORNBREAD AND APPLE RINGS

The classic pairing of pork and apples is found in this variation.

1 Strip the leaves from 3-4 sprigs of fresh sage. Finely chop the leaves.
2 Make the cornbread and stuffing as directed, adding the chopped sage with the pecan nuts.
3 Stuff and cook the pork as directed, adding 2 peeled, cored, and chopped tart apples to the casserole 30 minutes before the end of cooking.
4 While the pork is cooking, core 2 medium apples and cut them into medium rings, with the skin.
5 Heat 30 g (1 oz) butter in a frying pan, add the apple rings, and sprinkle each side with 15 ml (1 tbsp) caster sugar. Sauté, turning once, until caramelized, 3-5 minutes; set aside.
6 Transfer the noisettes to a warmed plate, cover, and keep warm. Discard excess fat from the casserole; heat and boil the juices until reduced by half. Add the white wine, 15-30 ml (1-2 tbsp) caster sugar, salt, and pepper. Cook until slightly thickened, 3-5 minutes. Stir in 60 ml (4 tbsp) double cream, and bring just to a boil. Transfer to a food processor or blender and purée until smooth. Reheat and taste for seasoning.
7 Serve individual noisettes with a little sauce poured over. Serve with the reserved cornbread, cut with a "daisy" pastry cutter if you like. Garnish with the apple rings, and fresh sage leaves.

STEAK AND WILD MUSHROOM PIE

¶◉៕ SERVES 4-6 ⤵ WORK TIME 50-55 MINUTES* ♨ COOKING TIME 2½-3 HOURS

EQUIPMENT

wooden spoon

large metal spoon

fork

chef's knife

sieve

small knife

pie funnel**

2 round-bladed knives

pastry brush

oval pie dish (2 litre/3 pint capacity)

paper towels

bowls   plate

rolling pin

flameproof casserole with lid

chopping board

** demitasse cup or egg cup can also be used

A departure from the familiar steak and kidney pie, this version combines braising steak with wild mushrooms under a quick puff pastry crust. The steak is cubed and sautéed, then slowly simmered with the wild mushrooms in a dark sauce. A deep quiche dish can be substituted for the classic oval pie dish, in which case you will need to increase the dough quantities by half.

GETTING AHEAD

The pie can be baked 1 day ahead and kept, covered, in the refrigerator. Reheat it in a 170°C (325°F, Gas 3) oven just before serving.

* plus 1¼ hours chilling time

metric	SHOPPING LIST	imperial
500 g	fresh shiitake or oyster mushrooms, or 75 g (2½ oz) dried wild mushrooms	1 lb
4	shallots	4
6	sprigs of parsley	6
1 kg	braising steak	2 lb
35 g	plain flour	1¼ oz
900 ml	beef stock or water, more if needed	1½ pints
	salt and pepper	
For the quick puff pastry		
250 g	plain flour, more for sprinkling	8 oz
175 g	unsalted butter	6 oz
100 ml	water, more if needed	3½ fl oz
1	egg for glazing	1

INGREDIENTS

braising steak

fresh wild mushrooms***   unsalted butter

parsley

beef stock   shallots

plain flour

egg

*** dried wild mushrooms can also be used

ORDER OF WORK

1 **MAKE THE QUICK PUFF PASTRY**

2 **PREPARE THE STEAK AND MUSHROOM FILLING**

3 **FINISH AND BAKE THE PIE**

1 MAKE THE QUICK PUFF PASTRY

1 Sift the flour and 2.5 ml (½ tsp) salt into a large bowl. Add one-third of the butter to the bowl and cut it into the flour with the round-bladed knives to form coarse crumbs.

2 Make a well in the centre of the flour and butter mixture and pour the water into the well.

3 Draw in the flour and mix to a rough dough. If the dough is dry, add a little more water. Press the dough into a ball. Wrap it tightly and chill 15 minutes.

4 Roll out the dough on a lightly floured surface to a 15 x 38 cm (6 x 15 inch) rectangle. Cut the remaining butter into small pieces, then dot the pieces over two-thirds of the dough rectangle.

Dot butter over two-thirds of dough

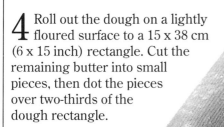

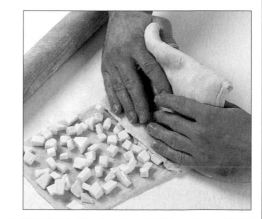

5 Fold the unbuttered dough over half of the buttered portion.

6 With both hands, fold the dough again so the butter pieces are completely enclosed in layers of dough.

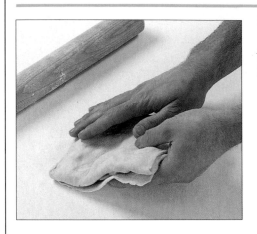

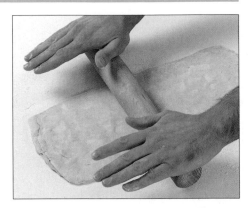

7 Turn the folded dough over and press the edges with the rolling pin to seal. Wrap and chill the dough 15 minutes.

8 Roll out the dough to a 15 x 45 cm (6 x 18 inch) rectangle, keeping the corners square.

! TAKE CARE !
Work quickly, moving the dough on the floured surface so that it does not stick.

Butter will be distributed more evenly by each rolling

Lift dough with both hands to fold

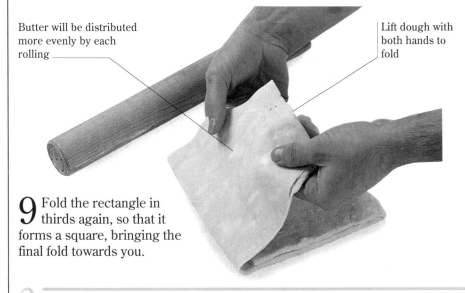

9 Fold the rectangle in thirds again, so that it forms a square, bringing the final fold towards you.

10 Turn the dough 90° so that the folded edge is to your left. Gently press the seams with the rolling pin to seal. This completes the first "turn". Repeat from step 8, to complete a second turn, then wrap the dough tightly and chill 15 minutes. Give the dough 2 more turns and chill again 15 minutes.

2 PREPARE THE STEAK AND MUSHROOM FILLING

Hold mushrooms stalk-side down for slicing

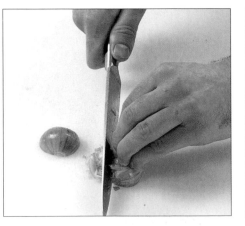

1 Heat the oven to 180°C (350°F, Gas 4). Wipe fresh mushrooms with a damp paper towel and trim the stalks. Cut them into medium slices. If using dried mushrooms, soak in a bowl of warm water until plump, about 30 minutes. Drain thoroughly and continue as for fresh mushrooms.

2 Peel the shallots, leaving a little of the root attached, and cut in half. Set each half flat-side down on the chopping board and slice horizontally towards the root, leaving the slices attached at the root. Slice vertically, again leaving the root end uncut, then cut across the shallot to make fine dice.

3 Strip the parsley leaves from the stalks and pile the leaves on the chopping board. Holding a few of the leaves together with one hand, finely chop the leaves using the chef's knife.

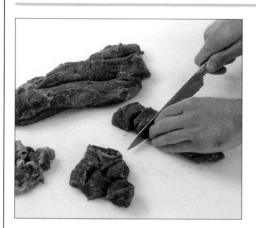

4 Trim any fat and sinew from the braising steak. Cut the meat into 2.5 cm (1 inch) cubes.

5 Season the flour with salt and pepper. Toss the steak in the flour to coat it, discarding the excess.

Coat meat cubes lightly and evenly with flour

6 Put the floured cubes of braising steak in the casserole. Pour in the beef stock.

7 Add the sliced wild mushrooms and chopped shallots and stir well to mix. Bring to a boil on top of the stove, stirring the mixture constantly.

8 Cover the casserole and transfer to the heated oven. Cook, stirring occasionally, until the meat is tender enough to crush with your finger and the sauce is the consistency of single cream, 2-2¼ hours.

Crush meat against wooden spoon to test for tenderness

ANNE SAYS
"The meat should be almost covered with gravy. If necessary, add additional stock or water during cooking."

9 Stir in the chopped parsley and season to taste with salt and pepper. Spoon the pie filling into the pie dish with the funnel in the centre. Let cool completely. Increase the oven heat to 220°C (425°F, Gas 7).

3 FINISH AND BAKE THE PIE

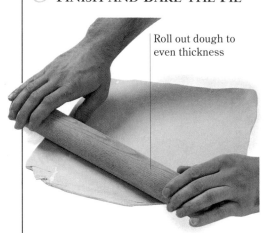

Roll out dough to even thickness

1 Lightly flour the work surface and roll out three-quarters of the chilled dough to a rough oval or circle at least 2.5 cm (1 inch) larger than the dish. Trim the edges and cut a strip the width of the dish rim from the edge of the dough.

2 Using the pastry brush, brush the flat rim of the pie dish with a little water, just to moisten.

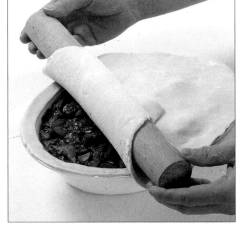

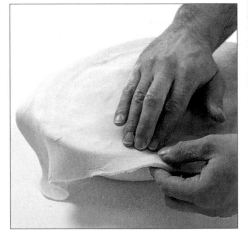

3 Lay the strip of dough on the rim of the dish and press it down onto the rim. Lightly beat the egg with 2.5 ml (½ tsp) salt for the glaze. Brush the strip of dough with egg glaze.

ANNE SAYS
"It's easier if you cut the strip of dough in half and then press on one piece of the dough at a time."

4 Roll the large piece of dough around the rolling pin and drape it over the pie.

! TAKE CARE !
Do not stretch the dough.

5 With your fingertips, press the dough firmly to seal it to the strip of dough on the rim of the pie dish.

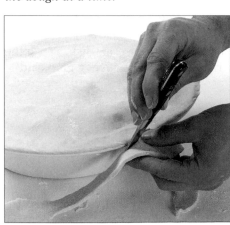

6 Trim off any excess dough with the small knife to make a neat finish.

Egg glaze will give golden finish

Use tip of small knife to cut steam hole in dough lid

7 Brush the top of the pie with the egg glaze. Cut a hole in the centre of the dough lid, over the funnel, to allow steam to escape.

Use back of knife blade to mark leaf veins

8 Roll out the remaining dough and cut it into 2.5 cm (1 inch) strips. Cut across the dough strips diagonally to make leaf shapes. Mark veins on the leaves and curve them with your fingers.

9 Arrange the leaves on top of the pie and brush them with egg glaze. Chill the pie 15 minutes, then bake it in the heated oven until the top is golden brown, 25-35 minutes. If the top browns too quickly, cover it with foil.

¶◉¶ TO SERVE
Serve the pie hot from the dish. Cut the crust in wedges and scoop out the filling with a spoon.

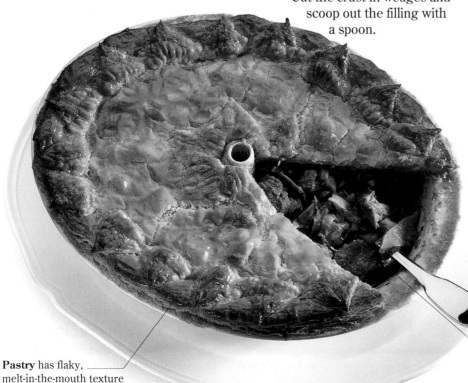

Pastry has flaky, melt-in-the-mouth texture

V A R I A T I O N

INDIVIDUAL VICTORIAN STEAK AND KIDNEY PIES

Kidneys and oysters are added to the steak instead of wild mushrooms in these hearty and delicious pies.

1 Prepare the quick puff pastry as directed in the main recipe.
2 Peel the covering skin from 250 g (8 oz) beef or lamb kidneys. Cut the ducts from the centre of each kidney and cut into 1 cm (1/2 inch) cubes.
3 Prepare the shallots and parsley as directed; omit the mushrooms.
4 Prepare the braising steak as directed and add 500 ml (16 fl oz) beef stock or water to the floured steak cubes in the casserole. Add the shallots and kidneys and cook as directed.
5 When the meat is very tender, stir in a dozen shelled medium oysters with their juice. Divide the mixture equally among 4 individual casserole dishes and let cool completely.
6 Roll out the puff pastry dough and cut out 4 rounds, each 1 cm (1/2 inch) bigger than a casserole dish. Brush the rim of each dish with egg glaze and top with the dough rounds, draping the dough over the edge of the dish and pressing it well over the rim to seal so it does not shrink during cooking.
7 Decorate the pies with dough flowers and crescents and bake as directed, allowing 20-25 minutes.

Wild mushrooms add depth of flavour to filling

Hungarian Beef Goulash

EQUIPMENT

chef's knife

kitchen scissors   small knife

wooden spoon

fork

2-pronged fork

small saucepan

bowls   2 teaspoons

aluminium foil

slotted spoon

flameproof casserole with lid

chopping board

Authentic goulash is half soup, half stew, made with beef and flavoured with paprika, garlic, and peppers. True Hungarian paprika, aromatic and piquant, makes a great difference to this dish and can be found in specialist food shops. If it is not available, you may want to add more paprika to your taste with the onions.

GETTING AHEAD

The goulash can be made up to 2 days ahead and the flavour will mellow. Keep it, covered, in the refrigerator and reheat it on top of the stove.

metric	SHOPPING LIST	imperial
6	onions, total weight about 750 g (1½ lb)	6
2	garlic cloves	2
60 g	smoked bacon	2 oz
15 ml	vegetable oil	1 tbsp
750 g	braising steak	1½ lb
30 ml	paprika	2 tbsp
2.5 ml	caraway seeds	½ tsp
500 ml	water, more if needed	16 fl oz
2	tomatoes	2
2	green peppers	2
	salt and pepper	
125 ml	soured cream (optional)	4 fl oz
For the little dumplings		
1	egg	1
45 g	plain flour	1½ oz

INGREDIENTS

caraway seeds

braising steak

smoked bacon

soured cream (optional)

vegetable oil

plain flour

tomatoes

egg

garlic cloves

onions   paprika   green peppers

ANNE SAYS

"Two types of paprika are commonly available. Hot paprika is piquant and robust, while mild paprika gives a mellow, sweeter flavour."

ORDER OF WORK

1 COOK THE GOULASH

2 FINISH THE GOULASH

3 PREPARE AND COOK THE DUMPLINGS

1 COOK THE GOULASH

1 Peel the onions and cut in half. Slice each half horizontally, then vertically. Cut across to make dice. Set the flat side of the chef's knife on top of each garlic clove and strike it with your fist. Peel and finely chop the garlic.

Stir bacon so pieces brown evenly

2 Dice the bacon. Heat the oil in the casserole, add the bacon, and cook, stirring, until it is lightly browned and the bacon fat is rendered (melted down), 3-5 minutes. Stir in the onions.

3 Cut a piece of foil to fit inside the casserole, then cover the mixture and add the lid. Cook over low heat, stirring occasionally, until the onions are soft and translucent, 20-25 minutes. Do not let the onions burn.

4 Meanwhile, heat the oven to 180°C (350°F, Gas 4). Trim the beef and cut it into 4 cm (1½ inch) strips, then across into 4 cm (1½ inch) cubes.

5 Stir the paprika into the onions and bacon and cook 2 minutes longer.

! TAKE CARE !
Do not let the paprika scorch.

Hungarian paprika has deep red colour

6 Add the braising steak, garlic, caraway seeds, and water to the casserole and stir to combine.

HOW TO CORE AND DESEED A PEPPER AND CUT IT INTO STRIPS OR DICE

The core and seeds of peppers must always be discarded.

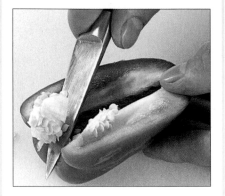

1 With a small knife, cut around the pepper core and pull it out. Halve the pepper lengthwise and scrape out the seeds. Cut away the white ribs on the inside.

2 Set each pepper half cut-side down on the work surface and press down with the heel of your hand to flatten it.

3 With a chef's knife, slice the pepper half lengthwise into strips. For dice, gather the strips together in a pile and cut across into squares.

7 Bring to a boil, stirring well, then cover with the lid and transfer to the heated oven. Cook until the beef is almost tender when pierced with the 2-pronged fork, 1-1½ hours. Stir occasionally, adding more water if the onions start to stick.

Heat goulash to boiling on top of stove before transferring to oven

FINISH THE GOULASH

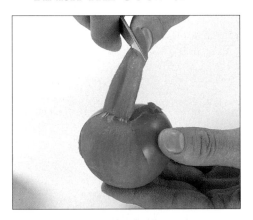

1 Cut the cores from the tomatoes and score an "x" on the base of each with the tip of a knife. Immerse them in a pan of boiling water until the skin starts to split, 8-15 seconds. Using the slotted spoon, transfer the tomatoes at once to a bowl of cold water. When cold, peel off the skin. Cut the tomatoes crosswise in half and squeeze out the seeds; chop each half.

2 Core and deseed the green peppers and cut them into strips (see box, left). Stir the green peppers and tomatoes into the goulash. Season to taste with salt and pepper.

3 Cover and continue cooking until the meat is very soft and the stew is rich and thick, 30-45 minutes longer. Taste the stew for seasoning.

3 PREPARE AND COOK THE DUMPLINGS

Take care to mix batter gently

1 Lightly beat the egg in a small bowl. Put the flour and a pinch of salt in another small bowl; stir in the egg.

! TAKE CARE !
Do not overmix the batter because this will make the dumplings tough.

Overmixed batter has elastic consistency

2 Transfer the goulash to the top of the stove and heat to boiling. Using the 2 teaspoons, drop spoonfuls of the dumpling mixture into the goulash and simmer until cooked through, 5-7 minutes.

🍴 TO SERVE
Ladle the goulash and dumplings into warmed individual soup bowls. Top each serving with a spoonful of soured cream, if you like.

Little dumplings are simmered on top of succulent stew just before serving

V A R I A T I O N

HUNGARIAN VEAL GOULASH

Cubes of veal are the basis for this goulash, with potatoes added for body.

1 Substitute 750 g (1½ lb) lean boneless stewing veal for the braising steak and cook it with the onions, garlic, and caraway seeds as directed.

2 Meanwhile, peel 3 medium potatoes (choose potatoes of a similar size, total weight about 500 g/1 lb). Square off the sides, then cut each potato vertically into 2 cm (³/₄ inch) slices. Stack the slices and cut into 2 cm (³/₄ inch) strips. Gather the strips together into a pile and slice them evenly into dice.
3 Add the potatoes to the casserole with the green peppers and tomatoes. Continue cooking until they are tender and the meat is very soft, 45-60 minutes. Omit the dumplings.

MEAT KNOW-HOW

What we call meat is muscle tissue. The harder the muscle works, the tougher it is. Tender meat comes from young animals, or from the less active parts of older animals, such as the hindquarters, the loin, and particularly the tenderloin or fillet (which is protected by the ribs and hardly moves at all). However, youth or inactivity are not in themselves decisive indicators of quality – immature meat can be bland, while the tenderloin and other inactive muscles tend to have less flavour than tougher meat.

CHOOSING AND SERVING

There are a few general rules for selecting all meat. Look for good butchering (a skilled meat cutter follows the contours of muscle and bone), with small cuts sliced evenly or in uniform pieces so that they will cook at the same speed. Cuts should be trimmed of sinew, leaving just enough fat to keep the flesh moist. Marbling is the key to the flavour and

tenderness of meat. Veal and baby lamb have little marbling, but older lamb or mutton, and to a lesser extent pork, should be lightly streaked with fat. With beef, marbling is a clear indication of quality.

Meat should have a clear but not bright colour: a greyish tinge is a bad sign. Yellow fat signals old age (except in beef from certain breeds, such as Jersey and Guernsey cattle), and dried edges betray dehydration in meat. Servings for meat depend on the type of meat and the cut you're preparing. As a rough guide for 1 person you should allow 250 g (8 oz) of boneless meat or 375-500 g (12 oz-1 lb) of meat on the bone.

STORING MEAT

At home, meat should be stored, loosely wrapped in plastic, in the coldest part of the refrigerator. Minced meat, offal, and cuts such as veal escalopes are best eaten within 1 day; chops, steaks, and small pieces can be kept for 2-3 days; large roasts will remain in good condition for up to 5 days. Red meats keep better than white meats, and lean cuts better than fatty ones, because fat turns rancid before meat starts to spoil.

An unpleasant smell, slimy surface, and greenish tinge are all danger signs that meat has been stored at too high a temperature or for too long and that bacteria have developed. Problems caused by rapid commercial chilling of the carcass, which toughens fibres, are less easily detected, although pallid colour and a wet package are an indication.

MEAT AND YOUR HEALTH

Meat, especially beef, has been criticized for its high saturated fat content; the highest grade of beef, prime, is the one containing the most fat. This had led to the development of leaner "light" meat with a greater proportion of lean meat and less fat. Cooking techniques that don't add more fat to the dish, such as simmering, roasting, and grilling, are another healthy option. These can be found in French Hot Pot, Roast Leg of Lamb, and Turkish Minced Lamb Kebabs. And it's easy to make other meat dishes more healthy without losing significant flavour. First of all, cut down on the amount of meat per portion and increase the vegetables; this reduces the calories too. Trim off all excess fat from the meat you use. Omit rich accompaniments, such as the Marsala sauce from Veal Piccate – serve the escalopes with the cooking juices deglazed with a little white wine. Omit the bacon, lean salt pork, and beurre manié from Provençal Beef Stew, and use a little arrowroot to thicken the sauce. When frying and sautéing, butter can be replaced with olive or vegetable oil, or with polyunsaturated margarine. However, pastry recipes will suffer in taste and texture without some butter content. Make these small changes and your favourite meat recipes will be healthier and still taste great.

FREEZING

Frozen meat varies in quality depending on how quickly it is frozen and how much fat it contains. As quick freezing causes less damage to the texture and juiciness of meat, smaller pieces freeze more successfully than large cuts. Fat gradually turns rancid, even in the coldest temperatures, so a lean piece of beef will keep better than a well-marbled rib roast. Careful wrapping is vital, not only to prevent freezer burn, but also because exposure to oxygen accelerates spoilage. Beef and lamb can be frozen up to 1 year, depending on the cuts, while veal and pork lose quality rapidly after 8 months.

For convenience, meat is best frozen ready to use as individual chops, chunks for stew, or patties of minced meat. However, very thin slices of meat tend to dry out, so they should be cut after thawing. Stews and cooked meats in sauce freeze well, but plain roasts and sliced cooked meats tend to dry out, even when securely wrapped.

! TAKE CARE !
Never refreeze raw meat.

THAWING

Frozen meat is usually thawed loosely wrapped in the refrigerator. Large cuts may need up to 5 hours per 500 g (1 lb), so allow plenty of time! Thawing completely before cooking helps retain the juiciness in meat, but if you must cook an unthawed piece of meat in an emergency, allow one and a half times the cooking time. Meat can also be thawed by immersing it, tightly wrapped, in a bowl of warm water.

! TAKE CARE !
Frozen meat should be cooked within 12 hours of thawing, especially meat stored with gravy.

MICROWAVE

Meat cooked in the microwave oven is often juicier than meat prepared in a conventional oven. Stews and meats in gravy cook to perfection. It also is good for reheating, allowing the flavour to mellow without overcooking. Keep in mind that a microwave oven works best with tougher cuts; more tender meat tends to dry out during cooking.

Defrosting meat is one of the great uses of a microwave, particularly for large cuts, but take care: some meats may thaw unevenly.

HOW-TO BOXES

*There are pictures of all preparation steps for each **Meat Classics** recipe. Some basic techniques are used in a number of recipes; they are shown in extra detail in these special "how-to" boxes.*

DECORATIONS FOR MEAT

The presentation of a meat dish improves dramatically with a colourful garnish.
I find that fresh vegetables are often the most eye-catching – here are just a few ideas.

HOMEMADE GAME CHIPS

Homemade game chips are an easy, delicious accompaniment to well-flavoured or barbecued meats.

1 Peel large firm potatoes (1/2-1 per person). Slice each potato paper-thin using the slicing blade of a grater. Alternatively, you can use a mandoline or the thin slicing blade of a food processor. Rinse the potato slices and pat them dry.

2 Heat vegetable oil in a deep-fat fryer to 190°C (375°F). Fry the potato slices, in batches if necessary, for 2-3 minutes until dark golden and crisp. Drain on paper towels.

3 Sprinkle the chips with salt and serve.

WATERCRESS BOUQUETS

Small or large bouquets of watercress make an attractive decoration for roasted or grilled meats.

1 Divide the sprigs of a bunch of watercress, then wash and dry them thoroughly. Align a small bunch firmly in one hand. Twist with the other hand to snap off the stalks and discard them.

2 Drop the leaves, stalks down, onto the plate to form an attractive bouquet. Alternatively, to decorate a large roast, use the whole bunch to form a giant bouquet.

SHOESTRING VEGETABLES

Shoestring vegetables resemble colourful spaghetti, good with meats in sauce.

1 If using carrots, peel them. For courgettes, use only the coloured skin. With a vegetable peeler or canelle knife, peel fine shoestring-like strips lengthwise from the vegetable.

2 Blanch the vegetable shoestrings in boiling salted water until just tender, about 1 minute. Drain well and add salt and pepper.

3 If liked, toss with a little melted butter, then arrange on each warmed plate in a small, neat pile.

RIBBON VEGETABLES

Thin ribbons of vegetables such as carrot, courgette, white radish, and parsnip make an attractive decoration, particularly if you mix the vegetable colours.

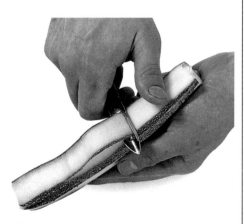

1 Peel or trim the vegetable, then cut off thin shavings lengthwise using a vegetable peeler.

2 Blanch the vegetable ribbons in boiling salted water until just tender, 1-2 minutes. Drain well and sprinkle with chopped parsley or another fresh herb, salt, and pepper.

3 Toss the vegetable ribbons with the herbs and seasoning, then arrange on each warmed plate in a small, neat pile.

TOMATO ROSES

Roses of spiralled tomato skin are a colourful and decorative addition to any plate.

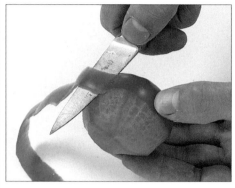

1 Using a small sharp knife, peel the skin from a firm, medium or large tomato, starting at the flower end opposite the core and peeling the skin in a long continuous strip.

2 Holding the flower end of the strip of skin between the thumb and forefinger of one hand and guiding the rest of the skin with the fingers of your other hand, turn the flower end to form a spiral or rose; hold it in place with your thumb.

3 Tuck in the end of the strip and set the rose on the plate to be garnished.

CARROT OR FRENCH BEAN BUNDLES

Carrots, cut into matchsticks, or French beans tied with a strip of courgette skin make elegant garnishes for meat dishes, particularly those with a sauce.

1 If using French beans, trim them to 6 cm (2½ inch) lengths. For carrots, peel them and cut into fine matchstick strips 6 cm (2½ inches) long. Cook the beans or carrot strips in boiling salted water until tender.

2 Meanwhile, thinly peel a strip of skin from a courgette with a vegetable peeler and cut it into fine "strings" using a chef's knife. Blanch in boiling salted water until pliable, about 1 minute; drain well.

3 Drain the beans or carrots. Arrange them in small bundles and tie each bundle with a string of courgette. Finish with a twist or bow.

INDEX

ACKNOWLEDGEMENTS

Photographers David Murray
Jules Selmes
Assisted by Ian Boddy

Chef Eric Treuille
Cookery Consultant Linda Collister
Assisted by Joanna Pitchfork

Typesetting Rowena Feeny
Deborah Rhodes
Text film by Disc to Print (UK) Limited

Production Consultant Lorraine Baird

*Carroll & Brown Limited
would like to thank ICTC
(081 568-4179) for supplying the
Cuisinox Elysee pans used throughout the
book, and Moulinex Swan Holdings
Limited for the deep-fat fryer.*

*Anne Willan would like to thank
her chief editor Cynthia Nims and
associate editor Kate Krader for their
vital help with writing the book and
researching and testing the recipes,
aided by La Varenne's chefs
and trainees.*

NOTES

- Metric and imperial measures have been calculated separately. Only use one set of measures as they are not exact equivalents.

- All spoon measurements are level.

- Spoon measurements are calculated using a standard 5 ml teaspoon and 15 ml tablespoon to give an accurate measurement of small amounts.